Our People and Our History

Our People and Our History Fifty Creole Portraits

RODOLPHE LUCIEN DESDUNES

TRANSLATED AND EDITED BY
Sister Dorothea Olga McCants, Daughter of the Cross

Louisiana State University Press
Baton Rouge

Translation copyright © 1973 by Louisiana State University Press
Originally published in 1911 as *Nos Hommes et Notre Histoire*.
All rights reserved
Manufactured in the United States of America
Library of Congress Catalog Card Number 72-79329
ISBN 0-8071-2740-X (pbk.)

Louisiana Paperback Edition, 2001

10 09 08 07 06 05 04 03 02 01

5 4 3 2 1

The paper in this book meets the guidelines for permanence and durability of the Committee on Production Guidelines for Book Longevity of the Council on Library Resources. ∞

For All the People of God

Contents

Foreword	ix
Translator's Introduction	xxi
Acknowledgments	xxv
Preface	xxvii

I
The Free Creoles of Color and the Campaign of 1814–1815—Hippolyte Castra — 3

II
Les Cenelles—Mr. Armand Lanusse and His Times — 10

III
A Dedication—The Collaborators of *Les Cenelles*—Some Biographical Sketches — 25

IV
The Collaborators of *Les Cenelles* (Continuation)—Biographical Sketches — 48

V
Beaumont and the Creole Song—The Toucoutou Affair—Poets and Journalists — 61

VI
The Creole of Color in the Arts and the Liberal Arts Professions—A Page in Our Political History—Popular Military Men—Figures of the Past — 69

Contents

VII
Music and the Creoles of Color—Rivalry Among Artists—
Prejudice   82

VIII
Our Philanthropists of the Past—How the Black Man
Knows How to Give   90

IX
The Creole Women of Color in the Catholic Churches—
The Generosity of Madame Bernard Couvent   97

X
The Emigration of 1858—The Politics of the Emperor
Faustin I of Haiti—Two Great Figures: Emile Desdunes
and Captain Octave Rey   109

XI
The Generation of 1860—The Hero, André Cailloux—
President Johnson and the Question of the Races—Our
Political Battles   124

XII
Politics and the Sense of Duty—Mr. Aristide Mary and the
Citizens' Committee—Our Last Entrenchments—Defections
and Failings—Our Last Thank You   140

Index   149

Foreword
Charles E. O'Neill, S.J.

In 1804 the French-speaking population of New Orleans addressed a memorial of protest to the United States Congress. Their language, a most precious possession, was threatened. They did not doubt that the time would come when their children would speak the language of the new republic which now governed their Louisiana, but they petitioned that there be no sudden elimination of the French language from the legislature and the courts.

In 1968 the legislature of the state of Louisiana passed a bill that assures the teaching of French in public elementary and high schools.

Between these two events lies the history of the striking survival to our times of the French language in Louisiana. The pen of many a historian and novelist has sketched the portrait of the French-speaking Louisiana gentleman, the gracious *châtelaine* of his plantation home and town house, his high-tempered sons and his vivacious daughters—*belles et chéries.*

What is not so well known is that many a French-language writer of nineteenth-century Louisiana was partly of African ancestry. Poets, journalists, dramatists came from among the *gens de couleur libres*—the free people of color—and their descendants. They shared neither the privileges of the master class nor the degradation of the slave. They stood between—or rather apart—sharing the cultivated tastes of the upper caste and the painful humiliation attached to the race of the enslaved. Little is known of their aspirations, their achievements, their anguish.

The "free persons of color" are found in French colonial Louisiana as early as 1725. On August 14, 1725 Jean Raphael, a free Negro from Martinique, married Marie Gaspart from Bruges in

Foreword

Flanders. On November 27, 1727, Jean Mingo, free Negro, married Thérèse, a Negro slave belonging to M. de Cantillon, with permission of plantation manager Darby.[1]

From then on church records and civil archives mention the presence of the free persons of color. Some entered the colony as free people, some were freed in recognition of merit and loyalty.[2] Some had been slaves, but had been given freedom by their white lover or parent; some had purchased their freedom by extra work during leisure hours.

According to the *Code Noir*, the free person of color had the rights of any citizen of French Louisiana, except for marriage with and legacies from whites. In a society where a black slave could sue a white the position of the free person of color was more solid indeed. Yet the social pressure of custom maintained the superior position of the white over the person of color however free and "equal." [3]

During the Spanish regime, easy emancipation prevailed and the free population of color continued to grow. The census of 1788 showed 1,701 free Negroes in a total population of 43,111 in Louisiana and West Florida.[4] In New Orleans their number grew from 99 out of 3,190 in 1769 to 1,355 out of 10,000 in 1803.[5]

While on several occasions the French had given freedom to slave volunteers in exchange for military service in the defense of the colony, the Spanish organized a militia composed entirely of free men of color (*pardos y morenos*).[6] They participated in the capture of Baton Rouge and Pensacola in Galvez's dramatic

1. St. Louis Cathedral Archives, Marriage Book I, 89, 140.
2. See Louisiana State Museum Archives, May 13, 1730, LHQ, IV, 524.
3. Paris,Archives des Colonies, B43, 388–407.
4. H. E. Sterkx, *The Free Negro in Ante-Bellum Louisiana*, (Rutherford, N.J., 1972), 85.
5. Lawrence Kinnaird, ed., *Spain in the Mississippi Valley 1765–1794* (Washington, AHA, 1940), II, 196.
6. Archival references in E. J. Burrus, J. de la Peña, C. E. O'Neill and M. T. García, *Catálogo de Documentos del Archivo General de Indias Sección V, Gobierno, Audiencia de Santo Domingo, sobre la Epoca Española de Luisiana* (New Orleans, 1968), II, 506. Roland C. McConnell, *Negro Troops of Ante-Bellum Louisiana* (Baton Rouge, 1968), 4–32.

Foreword

campaigns against the British during the American War of Independence.[7]

In the Spanish era (1766–1803) the free Negro enjoyed a lively social life in New Orleans. The city's first theater had mulatto stars.[8] The average white accepted this middle layer of society between himself and the black slaves, and dealt easily with its members. Yet the white population had two complaints. They suspected that the free mulatto might promote slave discontent and revolt. They admired the beauty of the cafe-au-lait quadroons and octaroons, but felt that the liaisons constantly undermined the morals of young white males.[9]

Revolution in Saint-Domingue sent refugees fleeing to Louisiana, white and black and mixed, slave and free, young and old. Cuba also sent emigrants to New Orleans in the first decade of the nineteenth century. By 1810 there were 7,585 free persons of color among the 76,500 who lived in the Territory of Orleans soon to become the state of Louisiana (1812).[10]

In 1812 Louisiana's Battalion of Free Men of Color was unique in the United States, the "only Negro volunteer militia with its own line officers." Andrew Jackson welcomed the free Negro troops who fought heroically at the Battle of New Orleans (1815). The state legislature gratefully praised their patriotism and bravery.[11]

Valor and prowess in the field did not win expected American rights in the constitution and legislature of the new state. Only twenty-one-year-old white males could vote and be elected representatives; as their age increased they became eligible for the senate.[12]

---

7. Sterkx, *The Free Negro*, 74. McConnell, *Negro Troops*, 17–21.
8. Rene LeGardeur, Jr., *The First New Orleans Theatre* (New Orleans, 1963), 10–14.
9. Sterkx, *The Free Negro*, 61 ff and 84.
10. *Aggregate Amount of Persons Within the United States in the Year 1810* (Washington, 1811), I, 82.
11. McConnell, *Negro Troops*, 53, 67, 70 and 99; Marcus B. Christian, *Negro Soldiers in the Battle of New Orleans* (New Orleans, 1965).
12. Louisiana Constitution of 1812, Art. II, Sec. 4, 8 and 12. Louisiana Constitution of 1845, Title II, Art. 6, 10 and 18.

Foreword

Political discrimination did not block financial power. Several persons of color amassed outstanding fortunes, particularly in real estate. However, the vast majority of this ethnic and social middle group lived by arduous toil in trades. Most typical were the occupations of tailor, barber, carpenter, mason, cigar maker, shoemaker and hack driver.[13]

Without ever according political equality the Louisiana Supreme Court steadily protected the middle position of the free persons of color against the more militant whites. In the antebellum era, a recent study concludes, "free Negroes [in Louisiana] can be considered as possessing the status of quasi-citizenship and as such enjoyed a better position than any of their counterparts in other states of the South." [14] Yet the free man of color continued to be "denied legal suffrage, the right to run for public office, and made the subject of discriminatory legislation because of his color." [15]

As the abolitionist movement intensified, feeling against the free persons of color increased. The fear of slave rebellion was ever present, and the free Negro was, in the mind of the dominant but slightly outnumbered race, the most likely leader of any such uprising. Thus between 1830 and 1860 social pressure and legislative action increased against emancipations, against immigration of free Negroes, and in favor of colonizing resident free Negroes out of the state. Finally in 1857 legislation was passed putting an end completely to manumissions in Louisiana.[16]

When Louisiana had entered the union as a state in 1812, there had been among its total population of almost 80,000 about 8,000 free persons of color; most of them resided in the city of New Orleans. When Louisiana seceded and joined the Confederacy in 1861, her free persons of color numbered about

---

13. Robert C. Reinders, "The Free Negro in the New Orleans Economy," *Louisiana History*, 6 (1965), 274–81. Sterkx, *The Free Negro*, Chapter V, "The Economic Life of the Free Negro."
14. Sterkx, *The Free Negro*, 171.   15. *Ibid.*, 199.
16. *Ibid.*, 119–50, 285–315.

Foreword

18,700, over half of whom lived in New Orleans; by this time Louisiana's total population had increased to about 709,000.[17]

During the Civil War three regiments of "men of color in New Orleans were the only organized [Negro] soldiery on the Confederate side." With what freedom and under what pressure they enlisted is not clear. Overconfident Louisiana leaders dismissed these militiamen as not needed. After the Federals took New Orleans in 1862, the city's men of color, jointly with newly freed slaves, composed the first colored regiment of the Federal army. Louisiana "furnished more colored troops for the war than any other State," but the majority of them were freedmen, who in the general population far outnumbered the "f.p.c." [18]

In the Reconstruction era, education and savoir-faire led the free persons of color into leadership posts ahead of the newly freed slaves. Active in politics and in the press, these leaders surpassed their counterparts in other states.[19] With anguish and dismay the late-nineteenth-century heirs of the free people of color witnessed the raging surge of the campaign for segregation and disenfranchisement. They—R. L. Desdunes and his friend Homère Plessy among them—did what they could, but they faced a tidal wave of emotions and laws.

Two decades after the wave had struck, Black historian Alice Dunbar-Nelson wrote: "There is no State in the Union, hardly any spot of like size on the globe, where the man of color has lived so intensely, made so much progress, been of such historical importance and yet about whom so comparatively little is known. His history is like the Mardi Gras of the city of New Orleans, beautiful and mysterious and wonderful, but with a serious thought underlying it all. May it be better known to the world some day." [20]

17. *Population of the United States in 1860* (Washington, 1864), 194.
18. Alice Dunbar-Nelson, "People of Color in Louisiana," *Journal of Negro History*, II (1917), 67–69. John D. Winter, *The Civil War in Louisiana*, (Baton Rouge, 1963), 35, 129, 144–45, 209, 253.
19. Charles B. Rousseve, *The Negro in Louisiana* (New Orleans, 1937), 96–125.
20. Dunbar-Nelson, "People of Color in Louisiana," 78.

Foreword

It was this abysmal knowledge gap which Rodolphe Lucien Desdunes had tried to fill by his major work, *Nos Hommes et Notre Histoire,* published in 1911. Black pride and French pride flow in his recounting of these biographies. Gifted, but deprived of higher education, Rodolphe Desdunes not only provides data unobtainable elsewhere but also serves as a symbol of the people whom he memorialized.

Little about him has been published, little has been known. Even the indefatigable researcher Edward Larocque Tinker had little to show, and that little was not entirely accurate.[21]

Rodolphe Lucien Desdunes was born in New Orleans November 15, 1849. Jeremiah Desdunes, his father, had been forced to leave Haiti in a political struggle. Jeremiah's wife Henrietta was a Cuban.[22] The couple had two other sons, Pierre-Aristide (a poet by profession, a cigar-maker by trade) and Daniel.[23]

Rodolphe married Mathilde Chaval, and of their union were born Wendell, Daniel (who taught music at Boys Town in Nebraska), Coritza, Agnes, Lucille, and Jeanne. The family lived at 928 Marais Street in downtown New Orleans.[24]

The family formerly had a cigar factory, with tobacco coming from their own plantation. However, jovial raconteur Rodolphe Lucien Desdunes was not a businessman; he wanted to write. In 1879 he obtained a job with the United States Customs Service as a messenger, with a salary of six hundred dollars a year. The following year he rose to clerk at fourteen hundred dollars a year. He was dropped from the rolls in August, 1885, an event perhaps related to the Republicans' loss of the presi-

---

21. Edward Laroque Tinker, *Les écrits de langue française en Louisiane au XIXe siècle* (Paris: Libraire Ancienne Honoré Champion, 1932), 134.

22. Certificate of Death A4339, Omaha-Douglas County Health Department; interview with Mr. Theodore Frere, grandson of Rodolphe Lucien Desdunes, May 2, 1971.

23. Edward Maceo Coleman, *Creole Voices: Poems in French by Free Men of Color* (Washington, D.C.: The Associated Publishers, Inc., 1945), 122–23. The late A. P. Tureaud, distinguished attorney and historian, enlightened and encouraged me as he did also the late Mr. Coleman.

24. Interview with Theodore Frere; New Orleans *City Directory, 1912.*

Foreword

dency to Democrat Grover Cleveland. Yet Desdunes returned to the service as clerk, to serve from 1891 to 1894.[25]

It was during this period that Desdunes, with a few friends, organized the *Comité des Citoyens,* Citizens' Committee, which launched the *Plessy* v. *Ferguson* case.[26] The 1890's were a discouraging decade, for not only did the United States Supreme Court uphold racial segregation in 1896, but also the state of Louisiana revised its constitution in 1898 so as to disfranchise the Negro. The personal memoirs given by Desdunes in *Nos Hommes et Notre Histoire* reach only through 1896.

In 1899, once again at the Customhouse, Desdunes was given the post of assistant weigher at twelve hundred dollars a year on a probationary basis. On August 5, 1899, he signed the oath of office in a firm, round hand. His conduct and capacity having proven satisfactory, he received a permanent appointment on January 31, 1900.[27]

Life seemed secure at this time for Desdunes. The Republicans continued to hold the presidency; Theodore Roosevelt succeeded the assassinated William McKinley, and then went on to win a four-year term in his own right. (Desdunes would see that a grandson of his was named for his admired President Teddy.) The former merchant, turned-customs-inspector, had a position with a solid salary that permitted him to write—like customs officers Nathaniel Hawthorne and Herman Melville of an earlier period.

Then one day in 1911(?), Desdunes and four other officers went to supervise weighing for customs aboard a ship unloading

---

25. J. W. Fath, Acting Chief, Civilian Reference Branch, National Records Center, to Charles E. O'Neill, June 8, 1971; interview with Theodore Frere.
26. Rodolphe Lucien Desdunes, *Hommage rendu . . . Alexandre Aristide Mary . . .* (New Orleans, 1893), 11.
27 Oath of office, August 5, 1899; oath of office for absolute appointment, February 5, 1900; L. J. Gage to Collector of Customs, New Orleans, Louisiana, January 31, 1900, National Archives, Treasury Department, Record Group 56. With gratitude to Mark G. Eckhoff, Director of Legislative, Judicial, and Diplomatic Records Division.

Foreword

granite. In a tragic accident dust blew from the stone into his eyes. Despite efforts made in federal hospitals to save the sexagenarian's eyesight, Desdunes was to spend the remaining seventeen years of his life in degrees of blindness.[28] He had to retire from the Customs Service in September, 1912.[29]

Still, he had his wife, his children, his grandchildren, and his friends. Dr. Dusuau, a pharmacist, used to read to him. René Grandjean used to converse with him. Grandmother Mathilde had goodies for the grandchildren, but the young people had to go outside when the patriarch engaged in long conversations with old friends. Desdunes wrote English with style and spoke it fairly well, but at home he preferred French. He liked his tobacco, a family tradition. Wine he took sparingly, a little with his meals but nothing more.[30] Such was the daily routine of this benign, dignified man.

His grandson, Theodore Frere, recalls a childhood memory. Grandfather Desdunes used to leave hanging outside of the house the gun he was assigned as a customs agent. Naturally the firearm rusted. Desdunes would say: "When I cannot subdue a man with my bare hands, I will quit, because life was given by God, not to be taken by men." [31]

While visiting his son Daniel in Omaha, Nebraska, Rodolphe Lucien Desdunes died on August 14, 1928, of cancer of the larynx. It was occasionally said that he died in California; this misconception may have arisen from the fact that it was Mrs. Coritza Mora of Stockton, California, who made the arrangements for sending the remains to New Orleans. He was interred in the family tomb in St. Louis Cemetery No. 2, Square 3.[32] His widow, two sons, and three daughters survived the venerable

28. Interview with Theodore Frere.
29. J. W. Fath to Charles E. O'Neill, June 8, 1971.
30. Interview with Theodore Frere.   31. *Ibid.*
32. Certificate of Death A4339. (On the certificate his "color or race" is listed as "French.") Tinker, *Les écrits de langue française*, 134. F. G. Rome, Executive Director, New Orleans Archdiocesan Cemeteries, to Charles E O'Neill, April 1, 1971. Desdunes may have been en route to or from California.

Portrait of Rodolphe Lucien Desdunes from the frontispiece of the original French edition of *Nos Hommes et Notre Histoire*.

Rodolphe Lucien Desdunes in his later years.

author who had celebrated the eloquence and the suffering of his people.[33]

Desdunes' literary career included contributions to *The Crusader* (1889–98), a journal published by Dr. L. Martinet. From Desdunes' pen came also some pamphlets—for example, *Hommage rendu à la mémoire d'Alexandre Aristide Mary décédé à la Nouvelle-Orléans, le 15 mai, 1893, à l'âge de 70 ans.* The eighteen-page pamphlet was "not for sale," but was distributed among friends. Mary's generosity as quiet contributor to many causes was praised. Desdunes told of how Mary had opposed P. B. S. Pinchback regarding the establishment of a separate state university for blacks, which would be called "Southern University." A visit by Desdunes had led Mary to lend his support to the fund that would carry Homère Plessy's case through the courts.

Tragically, Mary, a septuagenarian "hypochondriac," had taken his own life. Desdunes, annoyed that Mary had been refused church burial, complained that some persons less Christian than this *"libre penseur"* suicide had been accorded religious funeral services. He challenged his local Catholic clergy to see to the elimination of "unjust manoeuvers" and "affronts, even in the house of God." [34]

In March, 1907, Desdunes published a fifteen-page pamphlet entitled *A Few Words to Dr. DuBois 'With Malice Toward None.'* Acknowledging the position of the learned northern Negro academician, Desdunes was piqued by W. E. B. Du Bois' blanket generalization that the southern Negro lacked book learning and industrial skills. "The Negroes of the South do not deserve to stand under the indictment which the first part of that declaration conveys." [35] The New Orleans Creole Ne-

---

33. New Orleans *Times-Picayune*, August 17, 1928.
34. Desdunes, *Hommage rendu*, 17. Another eulogy by Desdunes, two pages of verse, was printed and distributed, *A la memoire de* [sic] *Eugène Antoine, Décédé le 19 Décembre 1905, a l'age de 61 ans.* (New Orleans, 1906[?]),
35. Rodolphe Lucien Desdunes, *A Few Words to Dr. DuBois 'With Malice Toward None'* (New Orleans, 1907), 2.

Foreword

gro listed learned and distinguished Louisianians of his race.

Desdunes went on to take issue with Du Bois' analysis and procedure in matters of race, history, revolution, and rights. He felt that Du Bois had uncritically accepted Toussaint L'Ouverture as the greatest black hero of the Saint-Domingue revolution, whereas, in actuality, he argued, L'Ouverture was quite willing to see the island remain under France and to accept a position of authority in the French administration. It was Jean Jacques Dessalines whom Desdunes considered the real hero. In a phrase that must have made Du Bois wince, Desdunes stated that Toussaint L'Ouverture was the Booker T. Washington of Haiti.

In strong terms Desdunes condemned white oppression. However, he felt the day would come when just whites would oppose unjust whites as in the days of abolition. "By striving for justice, justice we may obtain, by reaching out for justice and domination, we are in danger of losing both." [36]

Desdunes excoriated all flight from Negro racial identity. He felt that the present and future need of the Negro was a high moral integrity and a confident self-identity. This foundation he considered basic to political peace and happiness.

At the conclusion of the pamphlet, Desdunes posed a fundamental challenge to Du Bois' generalizations, for he distinguished the hopeful, philosophical Latin-culture Negro from the doubtful, practical Anglo-Saxon-culture Negro. Whatever may be thought of Desdunes' ideology, he shows himself in this pamphlet to be a reflective thinker and a well-read, scintillating discussant.

Desdunes' major work, *Nos Hommes et Notre Histoire*, had fortunately been completed before his sad loss of sight. The latest date given in the book is 1908. In 1911, L. Martin of Montreal urged the author to publish his manuscript and made arrangements for its printing and publication in the largest French-speaking city in America.[37]

36. *Ibid.*, 14.
37. Tinker's theory in *Les écrits de langue française*—that no Louisiana printer would have accepted the job because the book applied the term *créole* to persons of color—seems contrived.

Foreword

Keen feeling and simple manner run through his nineteenth-century style. The sophisticated critic will look in vain for embellishing conceits. His book was his avocation—a labor of love for his people. The data he was able to obtain are often anecdotal and uneven, and unevenly distributed, but his work is a unique source of information and insight regarding these men and women who suffered for race and for language.

Alcée Fortier, historian and leading connoisseur of French in Louisiana at the turn of the twentieth century, is said to have paid Desdunes a spontaneous if begrudging compliment. According to the etiquette of the day, Desdunes sent a gift copy of *Nos Hommes et Notre Histoire* to Fortier not by mail but by a personal messenger. As he leafed through the book, Fortier, a son of the "Redemption Period" in Louisiana history, was quoted by the messenger as having exclaimed: "Je ne croyais pas qu' à la Nouvelle-Orléans il y avait encore un nègre qui pourrait écrire le français de cette façon-là." [38]

I do not expect that spokesman-for-rights Armand Lanusse, editor Louis Roudanez, dramatist Victor Séjour, sculptor Eugène Warbourg, inventor Norbert Rillieux, philanthropist Thomy Lafon, social worker Madame Bernard Couvent, radical politician A. P. Dostie, or musician Edmond Dédé will ever become as well known as their counterparts of the majority-language culture. However, that they remain almost unknown is a national and local shame. The publication in English of Desdunes' tribute leaves less excuse for ignorance.

The French original of *Nos Hommes et Notre Histoire* is a collector's item nowadays. The translation of Desdunes into English by Sister Dorothea McCants makes available a valuable source book. Black and white, *Créole* and *Américain*, northerner and southerner, have much to ponder here of race and hope, of effort and disillusionment, of love of letters and—most of all—of neighbor.

---

38. Interview of Professors Marcus Christian and Joseph Logsdon with René Grandjean, New Orleans, July, 1970.

Translator's Introduction

In the course of a casual conversation on the Baton Rouge campus of Louisiana State University, Professor Edwin A. Davis of the university's history department called my attention to the current need for an English translation of *Nos Hommes et Notre Histoire*, by Rodolphe Lucien Desdunes. I was immediately interested in undertaking the project.

Nos Hommes et Notre Histoire—Our People and Our History—was published in Montreal, Canada, in 1911. Its pages record the poignant circumstances that marked the lives, struggles, and successes of an ethnic group, the Creoles of color of New Orleans, a group that rose to amazing heights within southern American society during the nineteenth century.

At this point I should offer an explanation of the term *Creole*. It is a word that was used as early as the sixteenth century to identify the descendants of French, Spanish, or Portuguese forebears living in Latin America, the West Indies, and in the southern part of what is now the United States. By this term such persons were distinguished from the native peoples and from immigrants.

Today the generally accepted definitions of the word seem to be in agreement. They concur in the idea that whatever racial elements are combined to produce the Creole, Negro blood must not be included in the mixture.

Some authorities hold that the word *Creole* is of Caribbean origin; others say it is derived from the Spanish word *criollo*, meaning indigenous or national. The Spanish Academy believes the word was invented and handed down by the conquerors of the West Indies. Those adventurers applied the term to persons born of European parents in the West Indies and also to blacks

Translator's Introduction

born in the islands, in contradistinction to blacks brought in from Africa. The term was unknown in Louisiana during the French period. Later, by way of distinction, the title was applied to descendants of the original French and Spanish settlers for the sake of convenience, and for this same reason, it was used as an adjective when referring to Negroes.

A. E. Perkins, citing Edward Larocque Tinker's novel *Toucoutou*, believes with others among his predecessors that "colored people cannot be Creoles save in the adjective sense, such as creole potatoes, creole lettuce, creole mules, creole negroes, creole anything produced in Creole Louisiana. . . . The controversy in terminology flows from the fact 'Creole' once had the meaning of aristocracy, culture, and exclusiveness among Europeans of Latin birth and descent in America." [1]

The New Orleans Creoles, who considered themselves as rightfully occupying the highest level of the social structure, were proud of their Latin blood, and during the late 1800's, "in their determination to repel all encroachments of the despised *Américains* they remained more French, James M. Barrie said when he visited the city in 1896, than the Parisians themselves." [2] Especially did they employ the term to distinguish their group from the Acadians (Cajuns), for they wanted no one to associate them with the French peasants of Southwest Louisiana.

In a like manner another group of New Orleanians came to use the word *Creole*. These were the free, mixed-blood, French-speaking descendants of immigrants from Haiti. Thousands of these persons were living in New Orleans and they objected to associating on equal terms with other blacks. The phrase "Creoles of color" was used by those people, who were proud of their part-Latin heritage, to set themselves apart from the ordinary American blacks, who could lay no claim to having either

---

1. A. E. Perkins (ed.), *Who's Who in Colored Louisiana* (Baton Rouge: Douglas Loan Co., Inc., 1930), 79.
2. Arlin Turner (ed.), *Creoles and Cajuns: Stories of Old Louisiana* by George W. Cable (Garden City, N. Y.: Doubleday, 1959), 1.

Translator's Introduction

French or Spanish blood in their veins and who could not understand or speak the Creole dialect.[3]

These Creoles of color with Latin blood, and certain other free blacks, made up a group known collectively as *gens de couleur libres*. This caste seems to have existed from the first introduction of slaves, and the *gens de couleur* were a part of the population from the beginning of Louisiana history: they are specifically named in the Black Code issued by Bienville in 1724. The Haitian descendants excelled as musicians, artists, teachers, writers, doctors, and in all major professions. Some amassed considerable fortunes and educated their children in France or in unsegregated schools. They were an integral part of southern Louisiana life and maintained their own social status with a rigidity as strong as that found among the whites. It is the stories of the lives and achievements of some of the members of this group that *Our People and Our History* unfolds.

Everyone realizes that a language suffers in translation, and certainly the French language does. I have made every effort to do justice to Desdunes' book, but in order to condense some of the material, certain passages have been paraphrased. I chose to give prose translations of the poetry selections not already translated and taken from another source.

Also, a serious effort has been made to identify some of the people whose names appear, perhaps once or twice, in the book, and who are only peripheral to the whole. These may have been other Creoles of color and residents of New Orleans, but searches of city directories and other available sources failed to turn up acceptable data in all but a few instances.

Sister Dorothea Olga McCants
Daughter of the Cross

---

[3]. M. H. Herrin, *The Creole Aristocracy: A Study of the Creole of Southern Louisiana* (New York: Exposition Press, 1952).

Acknowledgments

I wish to thank my many friends, both in Louisiana and elsewhere, whose courtesy, kindness, and hospitality so facilitated my work. In particular I wish to express gratitude to Sister John Roberta Sullivan, my Superior, and to Sister Clarissa Lacour for proofreading my translation and for contributing valuable suggestions. To all other Sisters of my Congregation, The Daughters of the Cross, Shreveport, Louisiana, I offer sincere thanks. I recognize the support and encouragement given me by the Church as a whole, represented in the diocese of Alexandria by the Most Reverend Charles Pascal Greco. I extend my thanks to Sister M. Reginald Warner, O.P., and to Sister Mary Aquin Loro, O.P., of John XXIII Library, St. Mary's Dominican College, New Orleans; to Mrs. Connie Griffith of the Howard-Tilton Memorial Library of Tulane University, New Orleans, and to her staff of the Special Collections Division; to the Loyola University Library, New Orleans; to Sister Stanislaus Dalton, S.B.S., librarian of Xavier University, New Orleans, and to her staff; to the New Orleans Public Library, with special thanks to the members of the Louisiana Division; to Edward Fontanette, librarian, and his staff at Southern University, Baton Rouge; to the Louisiana State University Library, Baton Rouge, with deep appreciation extended to Evangeline Lynch and her staff of the Louisiana Room; and to Dr. John Price and his staff of the Department of Archives and Manuscripts, Louisiana State University Library, Baton Rouge.

I am indebted to the Louisiana State Library, Baton Rouge; the Louisiana State Museum Library, and the Cabildo staffs, New Orleans; the Shreve Memorial Library, Shreveport; the St. Vincent Academy Library, Shreveport; the Franchise Tax

Acknowledgments

Board of Sacramento, California; the State Library at Los Angeles, California; the Chamber of Commerce, Montreal, Canada; and to the Centenary College Library, Shreveport. Grateful acknowledgment is given to Kathryn Bridges, Louisiana Librarian at Northwestern University, Natchitoches, Louisiana; to Marie Baboyant of the Montreal Public Library; to the Very Reverend Nicholas J. Tanaskovic, rector of St. Louis Cathedral and the record staff at the Cathedral, New Orleans; to the Very Reverend Charles Plauche, pastor of St. Frances Cabrini Church, New Orleans; to the Very Reverend Charles Edwards O'Neill, S.J., of the history department, Loyola University, New Orleans.

I thank Charles B. Roussève of New Orleans; Professor Marcus Christian and Dr. Joseph Logsdon of Louisiana State University, New Orleans; and René Grandjean of New Orleans. I wish to acknowledge thanks to the Very Reverend V. Liberto, pastor of St. Mary's Italian Church, New Orleans, and his staff; the members of the records department of St. Augustine's Church, New Orleans; Dr. Edwin A. Davis of the history department, Louisiana State University, Baton Rouge; Dr. Jean C. Brièrre and Thomas P. Fitzgerald of Shreveport; Dr. John William Corrington of the English department, Loyola University, New Orleans.

I offer deepest appreciation to all members of the Louisiana State University Press, Baton Rouge, with special acknowledgment of Charles East, director, and Leslie Phillabaum, assistant director and editor, and Mrs. Ruth B. Hubert, manuscript editor, and Ms. Beverly Penny, managing editor.

Sister Dorothea Olga McCants
Daughter of the Cross

Preface

I love the Creole of color. I love him above all when he is speaking my language. He is then somewhat a cousin of mine. As for the color of his skin, what does that matter? His father came to this country perhaps from Marseilles or maybe from Bordeaux. My ancestors came from Le Havre: Provence, Guienne, or Normandy—is not all of this France? No, I do not wish to pretend, as does the coarse Anglo-Saxon or the provincial Protestant, that my Latin blood has been tainted by a blending with African blood. Being a Frenchman, I find in the Creole some of my intellect. I sense my own feelings vibrating in unison with his. Being a Catholic, I recognize the black to be the work of the Creator, and, I confess that my share in the merits of the Passion of Christ is surely not greater than his.

I must add: When Lee's soldiers were surrendering their arms at Appomattox, I was not yet born. What I wish to say is, I hold no resentment for any of the humiliations or insults suffered by the black or the Creole of color some fifty years ago at the hands of Grant or Sherman.

I love my cousin because he knows how to love; I love him because he knows how to weep. The common slave does not know the meaning of tears. When he feels the lash of the master's whip falling more and more heavily upon him, he bends his back lower; that is all. This is not so, however, with the Creole of color, for I have seen some mothers furtively wipe the tears from their eyes as they told me of the sufferings borne by their children because of the injustice of segregation laws. I have seen strong men clench their fists and weep in anger at the thought of their utter helplessness to remedy the situation of their people. Then, more than ever, I have felt that truly there exists in them *half of myself.*

Preface

Several weeks ago when the author of *Our People and Our History* spoke to me of manuscripts lying in the recesses of drawers, I immediately begged that I be permitted the favor of reading and of bringing these writings to the notice of the public. Certainly, I do not at all regret having insisted on this, even to the point of annoying him, since through my efforts I succeeded in bringing the present work to the desk of the printer. I urge the reading of the book *Our People and Our History*. It is a story told simply yet realistically of the good deeds accomplished by a people close to our lives. It is also the story of their sufferings. Although born in the United States, these persons have not even been noticed, much less given recognition, such as that accorded the Barnums or the doctors Cook. They have not filled the world with the noise of their exploits; yet, we must concede they have exhibited a wealth of generosity and unusual initiative. In this, above all, they were French.

Rodolphe Lucien Desdunes in his youth did not have the advantages of a college education, because the doors of Louisiana universities were closed to him. Like all other Creoles of color who yearned to familiarize themselves with the beauties of the language of Racine, he had to become his own tutor. In this he manifested courage. He shows this same courage even more so today by his willingness to face the criticism—even the ill will— of the public by assuming the responsibility of undertaking so important a literary work as this is. The fact that he compiled this anthology despite the almost complete loss of his eyesight adds immeasurably to the beauty and the merit of his labor. Nothing stopped him in his effort to give us a knowledge of the Creoles—his brothers, his people—convinced that knowing them, we would esteem them more.

L.M.[1]

New Orleans, November, 1911.

1. Roland Wingfield identifies L. M. as L. Martin, but with no documentary proof. Wingfield, "The Creoles of Color: A Study of a New Orleans Subculture" (M.A. thesis, Louisiana State University, 1961). Charles Barthélemy Roussève, Negro historian, states that the author of this preface was a French Canadian. See Roussève, *The Negro in Louisiana: Aspects of His History and His Literature* (New Orleans: Xavier University Press, 1937), 23.

Our People and Our History

Chapter I
The Free Creoles of Color and the Campaign of 1814-1815 ∽ Hippolyte Castra

> *An injustice committed against one person is a threat against everybody.*
> —Montesquieu

One cannot mention the memorable campaign of 1814-15 without recalling the free men of color who fought side by side with General Jackson's other soldiers.

At that time there were three classes of people of color in Louisiana: the children of the soil, those who came originally from Martinique, and those who immigrated from Santo Domingo. All being Creoles, they lived on good terms, one group with the other, united under the same conditions: it was as though they had come from the same region and the same family. Resembling a group of people newly arrived together in a country, they formed one community, alike in origin, language, and customs. Above all, having been subjected to the same conditions in life, they experienced among themselves a strong bond of unity.

At the approach of the English troops [Battle of New Orleans], General Jackson called on everyone to defend his country, but he issued a special appeal to the men of color to take up arms against the enemy. His words of praise on this occasion left no doubt as to his feelings in the matter. He was convinced that the man of color had every right to defend his homeland, and that the American government would commit a grave error should it refuse to receive him under the nation's flag. This confidence and enthusiasm were shared generally by almost everyone.[1]

---

1. In 1814 Governor William Claiborne, seeking troops to defend New Orleans, advised Andrew Jackson to enlist the services of the militia of the

The famous soldier's encouraging declaration, accepted in good faith, aroused lively enthusiasm because no one doubted his sincerity. Consequently, colored patriots responded in great numbers. Their services to the nation in the Battle of Chalmette demonstrated incontestable valor. After the fighting General Jackson congratulated them, remarking that their conduct had far surpassed his expectations. But their recompense stopped there.

These men, whose fidelity and service had been so solemnly recognized, continued to live under all the deplorable conditions that the country had imposed on them, as though they had contributed nothing. They had to be content merely with the flattery lavished on them before the action and with the pompous but empty eulogies they received after the victory. Later these praises changed to ugly insinuations and malicious calumnies. It is therefore just that these unknown heroes complained of so much ingratitude.

It is true that in time the government gave them the title of veteran and accorded them a small pension, but their civil status remained the same. Through a modification of the Black Code, they were allowed the right to life, to happiness, to possession, to succession.

Because of his state of dependence, the Creole of color could not command the respect of his fellow men. He was, on the contrary, the object of hatred, contempt, and scorn. His so-called rights, revocable and tenuous, were subject to withdrawal at the pleasure of the governing class. Hippolyte Castra was one of these rejected heroes. He shared with his compatriots the bitterness of their experiences.[2]

---

free men of color. In his appeal Jackson reminded the black soldiers of their services in previous crises. He emphasized the need for their help, and he promised the members of the battalion the same treatment and rewards that would be accorded white soldiers. Roland C. McConnell, *Negro Troops of Antebellum Louisiana: A History of the Battalion of Free Men of Color* (Baton Rouge: Louisiana State University Press, 1968), 63–64.

2. McConnell states that it is impossible to identify Castra, as no such name appears on either the rolls of Major Louis Daquin's nor Major Pierre Lacoste's battalions of free men of color that fought in the Battle of New

A Tribute to the Creole People of Color

The people sorely needed a spokesman, and they truly found one in Castra, who may be compared to a Rouget or a DuBois. He used his unique talent to extol the courage, bravery, and loyalty of his brothers who had formed the black phalanx of the army. He sought to claim for these men their rightful place at the banquet of triumph, but recognition was refused them because of the prejudice that prevailed.

Indeed we owe to Castra a debt of gratitude and the best manner by which we can acquit ourselves of that debt is through the publication of the poem he left us entitled "La Campagne de 1814–15 [The Campaign of 1814–15]." We quote the entire text, just as it is found in our families' copybooks.

THE CAMPAIGN OF 1814–15

I remember that, one day, during my childhood,
A beautiful morning, my mother, while sighing,
Said to me: "Child, emblem of innocence,
"You do not know the future that awaits thee.
"You believe that you see your country under this beautiful sky
"Renounce thy error, my tender child,
"And believe above all your beloved mother...
"Here, thou art but an object of scorn."

Ten years later, upon our vast frontiers,
One heard the English cannon,
And then these words: "Come, let us conquer, my brothers,
"We were all born of Louisiana blood."
At these sweet words, and embracing my mother,
I followed you, repeating your cries,
Not thinking, in my pursuit of battle,
That I was but an object of scorn.

Orleans. And he feels that, because of the poem's subversive nature, its author wrote under a pen name. Nor can it be determined when (before 1840) Castra wrote the poem. It is not even certain that he perfected it: possibly Desdunes did so for *Nos Hommes et Notre Histoire*. McConnell points out that it is "one of the many Afro-French poems of a protest nature extant in New Orleans at that time." *Ibid.*, 106–108. Edward Larocque Tinker states that Castra took part in the Battle of New Orleans. Tinker, *Les écrits de langue Française en Louisiane au XIXe siècle* (Paris: Libraire Ancienne Honoré Champion, 1932), 74.

Our People and Our History

Arriving upon the field of battle,
I fought like a brave warrior;
Neither the bullets nor the shrapnel,
Could ever fill me with fear.
I fought with great valor
With the hope of serving my country,
Not thinking that for recompense
I would be the object of scorn.

After having gained the victory,
In this terrible and glorious combat,
All of you shared a drink with me
And called me a valiant soldier.
And I, without regret, and with a sincere heart,
Alas! I drank, believing you to be my friends,
Not thinking, in my fleeting joy
That I was but an object of scorn.

But today I sigh sadly
Because I perceive a change in you;
I no longer see that gracious smile
Which showed itself, in other times, so often
Upon your honeyed lips.
Have you become my enemies?
Ah! I see it in your fierce looks,
I am but an object of your scorn.

Translation from McConnell, *Negro Troops of Antebellum Louisiana*, 107–108.

Some Creoles truly think we should attribute these lines to the pen of Nicol Riquet,[3] one of our poets of *Les Cenelles* [*The Hawthorns*],[4] but we have no reason to believe that author would have produced so serious a composition.

3. Riquet (birth and death dates unknown) was a New Orleans cigar maker and poet. His songs were widely sung by the youth of his day. Only his "Rondeau Redouble" was published. It appears in *Les Cenelles* (pp. 75–76) and is dedicated to his free friends. Tinker, *Les écrits de langue Française*, 395. It is reproduced in the present volume, p. 57.

4. *Les Cenelles*, edited by Armand Lanusse (New Orleans: H. Lauve and Co., 1845), was the first published anthology of poems by Louisiana Negroes. It contains eighty-two poems by seventeen New Orleanians. Lanusse (see below, pp. 10–25) was a Creole of color and a native of New Orleans; he wrote the introduction and contributed sixteen poems to the volume. Edward Maceo Coleman, *Creole Voices: Poems in French by Free Men of Color* (Washington, D.C.: The Associated Publishers, 1945), v–xxi.

Edward Larocque Tinker comments: "Being wholly French in inspiration

A Tribute to the Creole People of Color

Mr. Riquet has left us the "Rondeau Redouble [Double Round]," a work full of lightheartedness. From all appearances his was a lively style, more inclined to bring a smile rather than inspire thought. Riquet was one of those "contented" people whose disposition inclined him to push aside all care in order to better enjoy the material pleasures of life. It is thus improbable to attribute to him the poem we have just quoted.

Hippolyte Castra

Moreover, men who have known Hippolyte Castra and who appreciate his literary contribution affirm that this great Louisianian composed the serious and noble lines found in that work. They regret that the poem was not included in *Les Cenelles*. The selection merits recording because it gives so accurate a picture of a cruelly frustrated people.

It is but natural that the author in the opening lines recall the prophetic words of his mother, "You believe that you see your country." Our hearts respond readily to the appropriateness of these touching words. In referring to the memories of his childhood, he recalls vividly the appeal, "Come, let us conquer, my brothers." Oh, did we not hear those same words in 1861, in 1865, and in 1898, and shall we not hear them again and again in other tragic times? Seemingly we are all brothers united as one in time of danger, but with the return of peace and security in our land, we fast become enemies.

Listen to Castra in the third stanza: "I fought like a warrior." All historical accounts agree to this fact, yet there was no recompense offered our heroes for the defense of their country. History tells us that the battle was terrible, yet our men went forward

---

and point of view, they [the poems of *Les Cenelles*] lack almost entirely indigenous flavor, and this coupled with the accurate and affectionate familiarity with French literature that they display would have made their genesis in any one of a hundred small French provincial towns seem perfectly plausible. Nowhere does it appear that the authors were colored, and it is only after this fact is known that it is possible fully to understand the vein of bitterness and the veiled references to prejudice that appear from time to time, . . ." Edward Larocque Tinker, *Creole City: Its Past and Its People* (New York: Longmans, Green, 1953), 268–69.

and "gained the victory." The poet depicts the conflict and the heroism of our men in vivid verse. He records how they fought to the death to obtain victory over the British, yet his country in return merely tells him he was a "valiant soldier" and drinks to his health in festive celebration.

The soldier suddenly sighs in deep sadness for all too soon he suspects a "change." He meets "fierce looks" and realizes that he has become an "object of scorn." This is the reward for his triumphs and his sacrifices. There is no doubt about the value of this poem.

Castra spoke about the misfortune of his compatriots; and his moving verses will always sadden us because of the circumstances that prompted them and because, above all, of the profound afflictions and bitterness that inspired them. The fate of Ogé and of L'Ouverture draws more attention than the color of their brows or the nature of their perilous enterprises. The same may be said of Pétion, the founder of the Republic of Haiti. People will soon forget the recent achievements of this young man who astonished the world by his wisdom and ingenuity. They will forget his prowess and remember only that he never gave cause for tears except by his death, for he went to his grave sad because of his inability to give to his people a stable government.[5]

The martyr Abraham Lincoln is another example. He was an idol of the American people. But even though he saved the na-

---

5. Jacques Vincent Ogé (ca. 1755–91) was a free Haitian mulatto educated in France. He organized a military company in the United States and returned to Haiti to lead a slave revolt in 1791. He was executed following his surrender. Benjamin Brawley, *Early Negro American Writers* (Chapel Hill: University of North Carolina Press, 1935), 262.

Toussaint L'Ouverture (1743–1803) was a former Haitian slave who rose to the rank of general in the French army. In 1801, as general in charge of the island's troops, he convened an assembly that adopted a constitution for the colony and made him governor general of Haiti for life. Napoleon Bonaparte had L'Ouverture brought as a prisoner to France, where he died. Roland Wingfield, "Haiti: A Case Study of an Underdeveloped Area" (Ph.D. dissertation, Louisiana State University, 1966), 34.

Alexandre Sabès Pétion (1770–1818) was a Haitian soldier and politician who led a revolt in Haiti, along with General Jean Jacques Dessalines, against the French. Pétion became president of Haiti in 1815, but died in 1818 while his government's financial affairs were in difficulty. *Ibid.*, 35.

A Tribute to the Creole People of Color

tion from the perils of disunion, even though he abolished slavery and gave freedom to some four million blacks, all of these good deeds combined did not win him as much veneration as did the pistol shot of John Wilkes Booth. Reason guides man; reason wishes that it be relied on at the prospect or memory of misfortune:

Sensibility is found in the soul
And the fact is compatible with misfortune that one experiences.

Chapter II
Les Cenelles ⁎⁓ Mr. Armand Lanusse and His Times

LES CENELLES

The volume entitled *Les Cenelles* is a small book of some 210 pages containing poems written by seventeen Louisiana Creoles of color. It was published by them in 1845. The book also contains selections by several well-known writers generally esteemed for their signal services in the cause of progress, justice, and humanity: Victor Hugo, Lamennais, Lemoine, Lamartine, Mercier, all Frenchmen whose genius and liberal views contributed notably to the progress of literature and society.[1] This little book, although rarely found today on bookshelves, holds an important place in Louisiana-French literature. We publish here the names of the collaborators in this anthology and give the titles of their respective contributions. Moreover, we present a poem by each of these men, with the intention of doing honor to their talent and of making available a book of verse for their descendants.

It is well to remember that the poems found in *Les Cenelles* were composed during the era of slavery and that those who contributed to the collection did not enjoy the same advantages as other men of their day because the writers were restricted by law and by social prejudice. From a philosophical point of view, *Les Cenelles* represents the triumph of the human spirit over the forces of obscurantism in Louisiana that denied the education and intellectual advancement of the colored masses.

In view of the circumstances and motives that inspired our

1. Edward Coleman states that the chief guides of the poets of *Les Cenelles* seem to have been Lamartine and Beranger. Armand Lanusse, editor of and contributor to the volume, turned to Lamartine's "pure and lively flame." Edward Maceo Coleman, *Creole Voices: Poems in French by Free Men of Color* (Washington, D.C.: The Associated Publishers, 1945), vi.

A Tribute to the Creole People of Color

forebears, this anthology comes to us as a sacred heritage. It is a duty of the highest order that we perpetuate the memory of those who bequeathed this volume to us. We wish, therefore, to save from oblivion the names of the seventeen Creoles who, at the cost of great sacrifice, left us this treasured book, because our people during this time were forbidden even to complain of their plight, of the civil, political, and social deprivations they were suffering.

We must add that the men who collaborated on *Les Cenelles* were the principal writers to come from the Creole population. At no other time have our people produced such a great number of cultured minds, and there has never existed a mutual agreement as perfect as that which united them in their interests and work. They were never jealous of each other, and they were always able to agree on the best means to use in order to bring to light the fruit of their studies and labors.

The authors were happy with the title they gave their work. The *cenelle* is the fruit [small berry] of the hawthorn bush: their small volume reflected the modesty of its authors. The hawthorn, "a thorny bush with both white and pink flowers," expressed, I believe, the trials of these men who were laboring in an environment so alien to their poetic talents. Trusting in the purity of their intentions, desiring above all to give *a bright aspect* to their unpromising destiny, the authors could not have chosen a more appropriate title than *Les Cenelles*.

Just who chose the title is not known. We know that the volume was published through the initiative of Armand Lanusse, but we cannot also attribute to him the choice of the title. The following lines preceding a poem by A. Mercier are perhaps indicative of the title's source: "Of all the fruits with which God has blessed our woods, happy am I to have chosen so appropriate a one." [2]

---

2. There were two Mercier brothers, Armand and Alfred, natives of France who lived in New Orleans after the Civil War. Armand, the older, was born in 1812 and died in New Orleans in 1885; Alfred was born in 1816 and died in 1894. Both were well-known physicians and practiced medicine in New Orleans. Both were writers of distinction and contributed effectively

In conclusion, if the spirit of the book may be determined by the arrangement of its contents, the beginning and the end, taken together, represent a significant parable, almost an allegory. We note that the first poem in *Les Cenelles* is titled "Chant d'Amour [Song of Love]," and the last is "Desenchantement [Disenchantment]." The two are by the same author [Pierre Dalcour], but this does not destroy the conclusion to be drawn from their contrasting themes.

Thus, in a passage from the first, the poet, full of faith in his ideal, expresses himself as follows:

> For only love, the love of a maiden adored
> Can console the heart with sorrow laden;
> Her love is an oasis, a manna consecrated,
> The source of pure water in a desert forsaken.

But much later, when "the dream fades in the face of truth," as Lamartine said, the poet surrenders to reality and believes no more in happiness. In his disenchantment, he cries out:

> My life of twenty years seems empty, dull.
> Already the flowers of my spring have faded;
> Already skepticism has withered my heart.
> Already, I have lost my faith in happiness.

Let the reader ponder for a moment on the difference between the first and last attitudes of the author. If we have not been misled by deceptive circumstances, the moral of *Les Cenelles* is clearly evident. These men of talent wished to emphasize that the sweet pleasure of any satisfaction realized by them could

---

to literature. Armand was one of the founders of *L'Athenée Louisianais*, and its first president, until his death. Alfred, the more prolific writer of the two, became a widely recognized author. While still living in Paris, he was French correspondent for the New Orleans *Daily Delta*, and he contributed to *La Chronique*. Edward Larocque Tinker, *Les écrits de langue française en Louisiane au XIX*ᵉ *siècle* (Paris: Libraire Ancienne Honoré Champion, 1932), 74.

Special reference is made to the fact that Alfred Mercier was a New Orleans novelist and scholar of note in Arlin Turner (ed.), *Creoles and Cajuns: Stories of Old Louisiana* by George W. Cable (Garden City: Doubleday, 1959), 7.

A Tribute to the Creole People of Color

never be lasting in a land where the liberty of some was not equal to that of others, where the individual born of a despised race and forced to conform to a set status would know only fleeting joys before succumbing to deep sorrow at the thought of his fate.

Armand Lanusse

> Men of justice do not fear
> the empty power of other men.
> Jean-Baptiste Rousseau

Armand Lanusse was born in New Orleans in 1812 and died there in 1867 at the age of fifty-five. His name at once indicates his French descent. Although this distinguished Louisianan received his education in his native city and did not enjoy the opportunity of being educated abroad as so many of his compatriots did, he was, in truth, an erudite man. He visited France only through the prism of his imagination.[3] In both his prose and verse, we find adequate proof of his broad education. He also delivered a number of widely acclaimed lectures. His poems, which have a singular charm, particularly drew the attention of his compatriots. He was blessed with a studious temperament, he loved the classics, and his poetry was deeply influenced by the spirit of these works. He was also very fond of studying the complexities of the French language and his favorite authors were such men as Noël, Chapsal, Poitevin, Lefranc, and Bescherelle.

Lanusse was a poet, teacher, politician, and patriot of the highest order. He was constantly occupied with all the questions concerning the welfare of the Creole population. His zeal and devotion in their behalf are among the best-known aspects of the history of our people. But in order to have a true appreciation of Armand Lanusse, it is necessary to follow the movements of his full and interesting life.

First, let us consider some of the tributes paid him by the stu-

---

3. According to Edward Larocque Tinker, Lanusse was educated in Paris. Tinker, *Creole City: Its Past and Its People* (New York: Longmans, Green, 1953), 262.

dents of the orphans' home [Catholic Institute for Indigent Orphans] where he served as director and instructor.[4] This conscientious and solicitous teacher lost no opportunity that could be used to the advantage of his students. As an incentive for serious study, the students were required to submit to annual comprehensive examinations; their parents were invited and thus could see at first hand the progress of their children. These examinations were festive occasions that extended over several days. The students' presentations ranged from samples of classroom exercises to various special recitations. Participants who were judged the most competent, the most talented, received public awards from the school officials.

Sometimes, on rare occasions, Mr. Lanusse expressed his satisfaction by bestowing a prize on the child who had received the most applause. We vividly recall Victoria Lecene, who was given such a prize. This little girl was truly marvelous. Her versatility, her talent, and her unaffected manner of interpretation in dramatic roles, all declared her worthy of her professor's splendid reward.

Mr. Lanusse was treated with deference because of his service, expertise, sincerity, and integrity. One of the qualities that proved the greatness of his soul was the liberality that marked his everyday relations with the world. It is said that he never once tried to hide or deny his origin, in spite of the light color of his skin and the oppressive times in which he lived. He was known to regard every man as equal, and he practiced this doctrine as director of the orphans' institute. He made no distinctions among his students based on the color of their skins, and the question of color never arose among them to disturb the calm of their innocence. As a result every student and faculty member was loyal to Mr. Lanusse, who taught us that

4. In 1852 Lanusse succeeded Félicie Cailloux, the first principal of the orphans' school, and remained in charge until his death in 1867, except for a brief time at the beginning of the Civil War, when he served in the Confederate army. Charles Barthélemy Rousseve, *The Negro in Louisiana: Aspects of His History and His Literature* (New Orleans: Xavier University Press, 1937), 23. Also below, Chapter IX, notes 3 and 4.

A Tribute to the Creole People of Color

> Vice alone is low; virtue holds rank;
> The greatest man is he who is most just.

Armand Lanusse encouraged his people to love their fellow men. His emotions seemed particularly aroused whenever he spoke of rising above prejudice and pride. Undoubtedly he believed that, after all,

> Riches and pride of life are naught but transitory,
> We are children of the same God, brothers on our journey.

We surely owe a debt of gratitude to this illustrious man.

In his introduction to *Les Cenelles*, he clearly indicates that he wished to be remembered by future generations as a man of good will. He was mindful of the words of Fénelon, "It is in truth a glorious thing to do good." Certainly Lanusse did ample good to merit the special consideration of his fellow men.

It is recorded that this man of love and charity possessed a violent temper, difficult to control, yet never in any way did he defend the dictator or the persecutor of the weak. Never did his impetuosity interfere with his recognition of what was right and just. He spent hs life fighting for justice, for the principles of truth and goodness. He spent his life fighting injustice, just as he gave of his possessions to help the less fortunate. His conduct, which was always in accord with the noblest principles, caused the men of his time to forget his fiery temperament and instead to love and respect him. We need a Lanusse among us to exercise the proper influence on our people so desperately in need of such a leader. Lanusse's powerful personality made our existence less difficult; under his benign influence, our community took on an air of honest industry and mutual cordiality. In earlier days our people were more strongly united by the bonds of love. At the present time, they are separated and torn by ridiculous antipathies and diversities of opinion.

The Latin influence among our people, in a sense, disappeared with the death of Armand Lanusse. With his passing away we are bereft of his example, of the stimulating force provided us by the classics. No longer do we occupy ourselves with reading La Fontaine, Boileau, Fénelon, Racine, Corneille. No longer are we ardent students of the masters. Lanusse led us in the study of these brilliant lights of civilization.

Such was the influence [of the classics] on our young people that they disdained the temptations of self-interest. Material pleasures had little attraction for those who had been taught that "neither gold nor the grandeur of this world can make us truly happy."

It may be foolish to dream of returning to those moral codes of living, but our people can be saved only by applying such principles in their own lives. They can never preserve their distinctive character by yielding to the inclinations of the present, particularly to the modern interest in politics. There is nothing in this new school of thought worthy of the name of progress. Trickery and fraud are now held as virtues. The revolting and pernicious examples of certain men ought to die with them— the men who recognize self-interest as law and who can serve as models only for people devoid of all self-respect. For us, rejecting the influence of the classics has meant condemning ourselves to live without the knowledge of certain principles indispensable for the formation of character. I have always believed that men of color should enter politics only out of a sense of duty and that they should never abandon their moral sense nor sacrifice their honor for money.

The power of the strongest men rises over the rights of the weakest. Under these conditions it seems to me that well-born men should refuse to participate in politics. The man of color who, despite the restrictions imposed on him, throws himself into political activities under the pretext of exercising his rights is liable to suspicion because he becomes the pawn of the dominant forces. I believe that such a role is not honorable and that the man who tries to fill it reveals the evil side of his nature and is acting only for personal gain.

It was as director and teacher at the Bernard Couvent orphans' school that Lanusse realized his greatest success. From

A Tribute to the Creole People of Color

1852 to 1866, he served on the faculty of this institute where he was instrumental in educating so many young people. Later in life these students distinguished themselves in the fields of literature, the arts, business and civic affairs. Most of these students came from poor families. Surely, without the assistance of Armand Lanusse, these boys and girls would never have had a chance to develop their talents and intellects as well as they did. This teacher did not consider the fees that he could have claimed for his services; he gave these children the same attention they would have received in the most pretentious schools either here or abroad. The excellence of Lanusse's system of education is shown by the ease with which his pupils assimilated the diverse kinds of knowledge they needed in commerce or in public service.

Professor Lanusse's task was not limited only to the creation of good scholars. Knowing that the institute that he directed was a legacy given by Madame Couvent, preferably for orphans, he dedicated all his energies toward seeing that her wishes were scrupulously respected.[5] In gratitude to her, Lanusse arranged an annual religious celebration in her memory. We recall how faithfully he would lead the orphans into the church to assist at those solemn rites. Today we no longer see this manifestation of appreciation. With Mr. Lanusse's departure, the idea of duty and recognition has also passed away.

Honest and loyal to the depths of his soul, Armand Lanusse depended on neither cunning nor deceit to reach his goals. Pursuing his ideals, he acted only with integrity and honor. There was nothing akin to luxury in his life. He tried to identify himself completely with his people whom he served; his ambition was to honor and to uplift them through his ideals and his labors. Time has proved that he achieved that end.

Mr. Lanusse's death came as a catastrophe. He left us at a time of civic and social transformation. Had he lived with us through this era, our people perhaps would not have been so misled as they were. Never would they have accepted absurdity and indig-

5. See below, Chapter IX, notes 3 and 4.

nity in the hope of escaping persecution. Alas, too many did so! Those are the ones who exchanged their diginity for a sham tolerance instead of accepting their share of the common suffering.

They would not have fled the scene of persecution nor would they have betrayed honor and blood. Rather they would have cried out with Pericles, "Honor is found in freedom and freedom is attained through courage." Or with Dr. Black, they would have exclaimed, "We shall die together!" We know this would have been Lanusse's advice to them.

D'Alembert was right when he stated that nothing is more cowardly than an oppressed people fleeing without resistance. This resistance can be sustained by the firm determination not to accept tyranny, even if one is obliged to submit to it. There is honor in suffering for what is right.

Everyone recognized such a determination in Armand Lanusse, and everyone knew him to be the enemy of prejudice. He could walk down Canal Street on the arm of his friend Mr. Louis Lainez, whose skin color left no doubt about his parentage, and command the respect of every passerby. That was because Lainez himself was an honorable man. On the other hand, Mr. Lanusse would not lose a day of his time in the company of some other blacks who had as much hypocrisy on their lips as they had hatred in their hearts.

Some Creoles in our own day have fallen to such a point of moral weakness that they have disowned and rejected not only their fellow blacks but even their own kin. These same people, far from seeking deliverance, surrender to their weakness, without being able to determine the correct principles to follow or to fix upon any resolution, as though they wished to accustom themselves to absolute submission or to forget their individuality. They live in a moral depression that seems to represent the last degree of impotence.

In this state of deterioration, they not only do not care to revive their fallen dignity, but they augment the sum of their errors, as if to multiply the number of their trials. However, it

A Tribute to the Creole People of Color

is not difficult to understand that when spirits are mastered by wrongdoing, when hearts are weakened by irresolution, hope loses its firmest supports.

With the aid of a compatriot like Armand Lanusse, some of our people had preserved their sense of unity. They did not run haphazardly in search of an imaginary destiny. This valiant patriot was blessed with both physical and moral courage. These qualities allowed him to master the most difficult enterprises and the most noble and efficacious resolutions.

There have been others among us who distinguished themselves by their valor. We do not wish in any way to detract from their merit, but there was a difference between them and Armand Lanusse. His main concern was with the formation of character, whereas the new leaders concerned themselves solely with the direction of our people in civic and political matters.

Armand Lanusse fashioned the man; the advisers of our people in 1868 sought to fashion the citizen. Lanusse's work was basically moral; their's was essentially political. The times were different.

ARMAND LANUSSE AND HIS TIMES   There is no doubt that the attitude of a group of people influences the deliberations and actions of its leaders. Mr. Lanusse's contemporaries loved such things as literature, painting, music, the theater, gambling, and hunting. In fact every imaginable pleasure appealed to them. And they unceasingly devised ways to create new diversions. This is why banquets, baptismal and First Holy Communion celebrations were so popular and so readily attended by our forebears. Weddings also were occasions for celebration. Games of chance were an essential part of every social gathering. People were not interested in the pressing needs of humanity. They did not seem to believe that the abolition of slavery would come as early as it did. Many persons of color owned slaves. The frequent and varied diversions therefore had little relation in our society to the question of personal freedom or the rights of man.

At this period in our history, people were most cautious in

their criticisms of existing institutions. The pursuit of personal satisfaction or the persistent acquisition of the material things of life occupied them. We find it natural therefore that Mr. Lanusse's literary works treat of the customs, feelings, sentiments, desires, and inclinations of his contemporaries. Finding himself surrounded solely by poets, this patriot was bound to be influenced by them. Obviously his desire was to see poets blossom in the future and not politicians.

And Lanusse could not attack the institution of slavery nor deplore its existence, because his friends said nothing about it in *Les Cenelles*. In other words he could in no way become an agitator, because he would have been the only one agitating. Too, Mr. Lanusse had no use for triviality: nothing made him more irritable than a pleasantry of poor taste. One day a friend who knew the serious side of Lanusse's character took pleasure in dedicating to him a poem he copied from a book whose title is unknown to us. A few days later, Lanusse's response was published in the columns of *La Tribune*[6] [*De La Nouvelle Orleans*]. We reproduce only the following four lines:

> God lives, you speak in truth; all nature tells us this;
> And the proof is as abundant as the sands of the sea;
> But if God is present in many souls,
> Satan, Hell's despot, in others reigns free.

We see here clearly that the Lanusse of 1865 was no longer the Lanusse of 1844. The influence of his milieu was no longer the same. The change in his society had placed its stamp on our poet. In 1865 we see in him a power, a thinking that bespeaks decisiveness. There is an independence in his style that reveals seriousness devoid of all thoughts of complacency and self-enjoyment.

Lanusse was first and foremost a Louisianian, somewhat in

---

6. *La Tribune* was founded by Dr. Louis Roudanez to promote the rights of blacks. It operated successfully until 1869, was the first black daily newspaper in the United States, and was the official organ of the Republican party in Louisiana. The paper and its staff are discussed in Chapter XI, below.

A Tribute to the Creole People of Color

the same sense that the citizen of Athens was an Athenian more than a Greek, or that the celebrated Calhoun was a Carolinian more than an American. One may say Lanusse never boasted of being an American. His pride in being Creole was more dear to him than his being a Louisianian, or than anything else pertaining to his origin. All his preferences and resentments stemmed from this.

THE COUVENT INSTITUTE Through a will drawn up in 1832, Madame Bernard Couvent had generously bequeathed certain funds and properties for the instruction of indigent Catholic orphans of the third district. The clause of her will that is of interest to us reads as follows: "I bequeath and order that my land at the corner of Grands Hommes and Union streets be dedicated and used in perpetuity for the establishment of a free school for the colored orphans of the district of Marigny. This said school is to be operated under the direction of Reverend Father Manehault or in the case of his death or absence under the supervision of his successors in office.[7] Also, I declare that said lands and buildings shall never be sold under any pretext whatsoever. Improvements or additions to the school according to needs of the times or number of students may be made through subscriptions or otherwise."

Through prolonged unfortunate circumstances, this legacy was left unused. A large part of it was diverted from the donor's original purpose. Barthélemy Rey, François Lacroix, Nelson Fouché, Emilien Brulé, Adolphe Duhart, and other patriots, having learned of the existence and abuse of this property, initiated a movement requiring the executor of the will to render an account of his actions in the matter. This was not an easy task, for twelve years had passed before the protectors of the orphans' rights thought of obtaining justice in the case.[8] Lanusse, although young, was caught up in the movement and, in the course of time, actively took over its direction. His energy, together with his intelligence, gave to the movement an irresistible

---

7. See below, Chapter IX, notes 3 and 4.   8. *Ibid.*

force that contributed much to the results it obtained. By 1848 the good work was saved; nothing could prevent the execution of Madame Couvent's wishes.

But this was not all. The properties had suffered from lack of attention and had to be restored to their former condition, and business affairs pertinent to them had to be properly organized so as to make them yield lasting benefits.

Lanusse again showed that he was equal to the task. He gathered together men of integrity and all began to work courageously. Within a short time they had erected a new building that they called the Catholic Institute for Indigent Orphans. The properties that comprised the legacy of Madame Couvent were used to sustain the establishment and were supplemented by additional private and public contributions.

It was but logical that in 1852 Mr. Lanusse be named principal of the institute. It was he who created the program of studies, it was he who put this program into action, and it was he who taught his faculty how to proceed.

To assist him in his work, he had chosen Joanni Questy, Constant Reynès, and Joseph Vigneaux-Lavigne, all men of merit and admirable devotion.[9] Under such direction the school prospered and became famous for the quality of the students it graduated. No longer did our people find it necessary to seek education in Europe or elsewhere. The program of studies at the Institute provided a solid education for all our people. Orphans and children of poor parents no longer had to dread the disadvantages of ignorance.

Mr. Lanusse was severely censured for not following General Butler's order to fly the flag of the Union over the school. We agree this was a mistake, but we understand too the challenge this posed to the conscience of so sensitive a man. Lanusse simply could not reconcile his thinking with such a gesture. We need only to recall that Lanusse had been conscripted into the Confederate army. Even though he cooperated and accepted the conditions that forced him to take up arms in the service

9. Joanni Questy is treated in Chapter III of this volume.

A Tribute to the Creole People of Color

of the Confederacy, he felt a distinct repugnance toward any public action at a time when political matters were in such a state of flux.

We hasten to add that much later he recanted his erroneous ideas and from that time on, his loyalty lay entirely with the cause of the Union and of liberty. It is known by all his friends that he deeply regretted the flag incident, and his loyal repentance should suffice to exonerate him. Moreover, the rest of his life proved that he committed only this one error, and no one could blame the motives that caused him to act on this occasion. We like to believe that public sentiment never reproached him on the subject of this seeming defection.

He was known to exclaim in 1861, "Shall we not go?" when our threatened people had to choose between exile or military service.

In a moment of what he considered justified indignation at the thought of being driven into banishment from his beloved New Orleans, he exclaimed, "Whoever looks for me will find me in my humble abode." To a certain person who declared that contact with a man of color evoked repugnance, Mr. Lanusse replied, "In you repugnance and instinct are one and the same thing." [10]

In his younger years, Armand Lanusse was particularly at the beck and call of his friends, aiding them in their modest plans and ambitions. He was also known to be a gallant defender of woman, let us say through a sense of chivalry rather than inclination. During this same time in his life, he was often seen at the theater enjoying a comedy with [Edmond] Orso, our noted tragedian. Still later he was upholding the cause of the orphans' education and promoting the church services held in honor of Madame Bernard Couvent. In the army he served more as a hostage than as a soldier. We read of him in books and news-

---

10. Lanusse was bitter against the southerner for holding his people in subjugation. Even after the Civil War, he advised all nonwhites to leave Louisiana for Mexico or elsewhere. He directed the Couvent school in a hostile environment, with his life in danger for promoting the educational advancement of blacks. Tinker, *Les écrits de langue française*, 264.

papers as a poet and an orator. He exposed himself to arrogance and conceit, always in the interest of education. Until his death he maintained ever the same image—the personification of sublime dedication.[11]

We can add only one other point to his eulogy: he was ever a good, virtuous husband and model father. Unfortunately, death separated him too soon from his family, whose help and mainstay he most assuredly was. Four sons and one daughter blessed his marriage union, but, alas, only one son survived him.

---

11. Lanusse was one of three free people of color named with fifty-two New Orleans authors in Charles Testut, *Portraits litteraires de la Nouvelle-Orléans* (New Orleans: Imprimerie des Veillees, 1850). The other two were Joanni Questy and Camille Thierry. Roussève, *The Negro in Louisiana*, 120.

Constant Reynes was a teacher; his residence is listed as Galvez n. Main. Joseph Vigneaux-Lavigne lived at 7 St. Anthony Street, New Orleans. *Gardner's New Orleans Directory, 1860* . . . (New Orleans: Charles Gardner, 1860), 232, 320.

Chapter III
A Dedication ❧ The Collaborators of *Les Cenelles* ❧ Some Biographical Sketches

Mr. Armand Lanusse had the honor of writing the following dedication for *Les Cenelles*:

TO LOUISIANIANS OF THE FAIR SEX

Graciously accept these modest fruits
That our hearts offer you in sincerity;
May a single glance from your chaste pure brows,
Bring unto them the glory of immortality.

Other writings of this poet that we have are: the introduction to *Les Cenelles*; the poems: "Le Dépit [Spite]," "Epigramme [Epigram]," "Un Frère au Tombeau de son Frère [A Brother at the Tomb of His Brother]," "La Jeune Agonisante [A Young Girl Dying]," "A Elora [To Elora]," "Les Amants Consolés [The Consoled Lovers]," "La Jeune Fille au Bal [The Young Girl at the Ball]," "Le Petit Lit que J'aime [The Little Bed I Love]," "Jalousie [Jealousy]," "Le Songe [A Dream]," "Le Prêtre et la Jeune Fille [The Priest and the Young Girl]," "Le Carnaval [The Carnival]," "A Mademoiselle *** [To Miss ***]," "Besoin d'Ecrire [The Urge to Write]," "Le Portrait [The Portrait]," "Une Mère Mourante [A Dying Mother]," "Il Est [He Is]."

Joanni Questy

Mr. Joanni Questy was born, reared, and educated in New Orleans. He was regarded as one of the most learned men of his time. Through his application to study, Questy mastered several languages; however, all of his known works were written in French. He was a refined scholar, and as an author his style is exquisitely pure and characteristically philosophic. Among the writings he left us, we find the following: "La Vision [Vision],"

Our People and Our History

"Causerie [A Chat]," and "Une Larme sur William Stephens [A Lament for William Stephens]," all of which were published in *Les Cenelles* in 1845. He also wrote a novel entitled *M. Paul* [*Mr. Paul*], but this work was never published. The manuscript is in the possession of Noël Bacchus.

Mr. Questy was an important collaborator for a number of literary ventures in our city. As a professor he excelled, displaying his talent as a brilliant teacher of Spanish and French. His career as a soldier in the army of 1844 is treated at length in another section of this work. Mr Questy enjoyed a wide popularity because of his amiable and sympathetic disposition. All the children knew him as Mr. Joanni [Mr. Johnny]. "Vision" was one of his first works. Its style is expressive, rich, creative, graceful, and spontaneous. Questy knew how to please, how to reach the heart. One may say of him, as Dumas *fils* said of Lamartine, that "his poetry was fragrant."

VISION

Come to me, radiant maid,
Come, goddess of the skies!
When lonely years shall fade,
'Tis thou shalt close my eyes.

Come with thy smile serene,
To soothe my misery;
For Heaven's wrath unseen
To woe abandons me.

Oh! come, each hour of pain
My wretched fate unknown
I weep, yet weep in vain...
None near to heed my moan.

Thy sylph I softly name,
Whose eyes of azure glow,
Who, rayed in golden flame,
Ethereal realms must know!

Rare maid from Heaven beguiled,
By hope and bliss made blessed.
On lowly earth exiled,
Come... lean thou on my breast.

A Tribute to the Creole People of Color

Who might thy father be,
Aerial child, pray tell?
What Eve once mothered thee?
Has youth ne'er loved thee well?

Mayhap beyond the skies,
Above the fleecy cloud,
Thy palace charmed must rise,
Abode of thunders loud.

There lyres celestial bear
Thee dulcet harmony,
Genie or angel fair,
Spirit of mystery.

Thy destiny's unknown?
Thou dost not answer me?
Must ever silence own?
Ah, speak! pray hear my plea!

Thou art the undine fair,
Of golden streams the queen
Mayhap, who deigns to wear
For me her smile serene.

Or irised gnome, to reign
O'er guarded wealth untold...
Of my poor, broken chain
Hast not the link of gold?

Tell me, art not the soul
Of the angel robed in light,
From a woman's arm that stole
And to Heaven bent its flight,

Ere dawn, but yesterday?
Perchance but lately dressed
Art thou, in bright array
Of throne or cherub blessed?

Thy destiny's unknown?
Thou dost not answer me?
Must ever silence own?
Ah, speak! pray hear my plea!

"Soul of a soul am I,
The lucid ray that fled
Through distant eastern sky
From flaming orb now dead.

"To the child sweet smiles I bring
Oft in its slumber calm;
When woes its sleep dare wring,
I waft a tender balm.

"From my bright crown I bear
Sweet flowers where'er I stray,
Where sorrows dwell, and care
Haunts lone and gloomy way.

"I bring to them that fall
In earthly agony,
Of death the secrets all
And Heaven's blessed mystery.

"In answer to thy plea,
Beside thy path I'll stand;
Forever shalt thou be
In the shadow of my hand.

Farewell: my crown enfold;
'Twill gage of love remain."
Shall I, blessed maid, behold
Thy seraphic form again?

Translation of poem from Roussève, *The Negro in Louisiana*, 74–77.

Mr. Questy wrote for *L'Album Litteraire,* and it is said he was the composer of the "Compliments de l'Année [Compliments of the Year]" for a certain New Orleans newspaper. *L'Almanach Pour Rire [Fun Almanac]* is also his work. In his last days he was employed by *La Tribune* as Chronicler.

Victor Séjour

Among the Creole writers, we pay special tribute to Victor Séjour, born in New Orleans in 1819. In 1836 he left his native city for Paris and spent the rest of his life in France. Séjour, like so many others, had to leave the country of his birth in order to throw off the shackles of racial prejudice. His father, a man of considerable means, operated a business on Chartres Street.[1]

1. Victor Séjour, Sr., former quartermaster in Major Louis Daquin's free black battalion of 1814–15, operated a drycleaning shop in New Orleans. It was he who persuaded his son to seek his fortune in Paris; there the younger Séjour gained entry into the literary field through his ode, "The Return

A Tribute to the Creole People of Color

Victor began his studies in New Orleans. He was an excellent writer, the author of several books of prose and verse. His poem "Le Retour de Napoleon [The Return of Napoleon]" commanded wide appreciation. His ready acceptance in the highest circle of French writers was proof enough of his genuine merits. In Louisiana his contemporaries bestowed on him the palm of excellence. Louisiana never produced a better poet.[2] He became a close friend of Emperor Napoleon III, who held him in high esteem. This fact was indeed a tribute to the colored poet and cause for legitimate pride.

Séjour was a prodigy. His contemporaries recognized this in a poem he wrote at the age of seventeen, a short time before his departure for France. Séjour was a member of the *Société des Artisans*. It was on the occasion of the anniversary of this association that he read to his fellow members his first creative effort. They say that this debut poem was a masterpiece.

The *Société des Artisans* is one of our old organizations. During this time there were certain class distinctions among the Creoles. The upper class, composed of professional men, wishing to distinguish themselves, had formed the *Société d'Economie*, which confined its membership to those Creoles with tendencies toward exclusiveness.

The artisans and craftsmen responded by forming the *Société des Artisans*. Séjour chose the latter. Undoubtedly his first poem

---

of Napoleon," reproduced herein. In 1844, with the staging of his first drama at the *Théâtre Français*, he achieved as a playwright; some twenty productions followed. Edward Larocque Tinker, *Creole City: Its Past and Its People* (New York: Longmans, Green, 1953), 265. He became more distinguished in this medium than in poetry. One of his plays, produced in 1862, had an American theme—*The Volunteers of 1814*. It was a five-act drama with fourteen tableaux concerning the Louisiana black volunteer troops of which his father had been a member; the play received favorable notice. Roland C. McConnell, *Negro Troops of Antebellum Louisiana: A History of the Battalion of Free Men of Color* (Baton Rouge: Louisiana State University Press, 1968), 105.

2. Probably because it was his only work of sufficient brevity, this is the sole poem by which Séjour is represented in *Les Cenelles*. The poem illustrates the sympathies and interests of Séjour and other free Negroes in antebellum Louisiana and their association with France. Charles Barthélemy Rousséve, *The Negro in Louisiana: Aspects of His History and His Literature* (New Orleans: Xavier University Press, 1937), 87.

was a satire on the bizarre conduct of those who disdained their compatriots, a satire against the members of the *Société d'Economie*.[3]

LE RETOUR DE NAPOLEON
[THE RETURN OF NAPOLEON]

I

As chafed ocean roaring 'neath a burning sky,
The people surged upon the place, their spirit high,
    In anguish crying: "Lo!
A bier!... O woe... for soldier hold a yawning grave,
Who lordly Rome's proud splendor to grateful homeland gave.
    Behold our all! O woe!"

When he, victorious 'mid our walls returned, and on
His brow the laurels of two thousand battles won,
    In artless grandeur rode,
This selfsame crowd, alas! his pathway pressed beside,
Hailed loud his coming forth, his valor glorified,
    And radiant in his splendor glowed.

Oh! then was France supernal, rayed in glory proud!...
She rose: the kings of earth in willing homage bowed,
Like ripened ears before the steady gale inclined,
As on she swept and on, a tempest raging wild,
The quaking world, by hope of triumph once beguiled,
    Lay low her course behind.

Now all is fled... all's ended... hail, O chieftain brave;
O hail, my consul of imperial mien and grave;
August and noble wast, supreme and glorious thou;
Didst Hannibal o'ershadow, haughty Pompey, too;
Thy saber's might all Europe proud obeying knew...
Shall narrow grave confine thy soaring spirit now?

Weep long, O nation, weep... behold him, wan and drear,
So like the icy pall that drapes his somber bier;

---

3. Black veterans in New Orleans organized themselves into a number of such social and benevolent associations; the *Société des Artisans*, for free colored mechanics, was incorporated in 1834. "Meetings of this organization afforded its members a sounding board for literary expression," for business considerations, "as well as [for] secret criticism of the power structure in New Orleans." The elder Séjour and his son were members. No doubt Castra recited his "Campaign of 1814–15" before this group. McConnell, *Negro Troops of Antebellum Louisiana*, 106.

A Tribute to the Creole People of Color

Weep long thy valiant Caesar, warrior bold, thy pride;
Weep long!... 'mid shot and shell, defending native land,
The soldier falls on field of battle, sword in hand;
    Thy prince a captive died;

Ah! pensive, lone, from Saint Helena's rocky strand,
When oft he gazed toward France, the distant fatherland,
    As toward a golden star;
And his brow glowed with some sweet memory's flaming light,
"My God," he cried, "I'd give my soul for one blessed sight
    Of France's shores afar.

"No, no, it is not I that Albion base and vile
Holds, like a captive lion, on this deserted isle;
    'Tis thou, O noble France.

" 'Tis thou, thy power, thy glory proud, thy destiny,
Thy twenty years of striving, thy years of victory;
    Not I, across this sea's expanse."

II

Then hasten; let him not, O France,
In vain await deliverance...
Lo, grasp thy shield, 'tis duty's plea;
Unleash thy fiery battle steed,
That vies the wrathful lightning's speed;
Go strike thy royal captive free.

Arise, ye people, loud the cry of battle sound;
Ye soldiers, grasp your arms, of yore with glory crowned;
    And in fair honor's name,
Let not our rightful wrath in silence, Frenchmen, sleep;
Two wait proscribed in Saint Helena's fastness steep;
    The emperor and fame!

III

Yet, no, too late... on modern Calvary's gory crown
Grim death has ruthless struck the towering figure down;
    And he is dead; too late!
O'erwhelmed, forlorn, betrayed by native land, he fell,
Low murmuring: "I die, O France I love so well;
    And, loath, I weep thy gloomy fate."

IV

His coffin's laid before us,.. blighting irony!...
Ah! Frenchmen proud, our honor writhes in agony!
For shame we well should blush; his very hangman wretched,

Our People and Our History

Lo, after sinking 'neath his feet a black abyss,
Now, glutted with the victim's blood, in brutal bliss
    To us as alms his corse has fetched.
For shame we well should blush, we nation great, renowned,
To dare approach the form of him that glory crowned,
    While insult brands our brow;
To dare, alas! our gaze uplift, when Punic palm
Yields his heroic frame, and, free from decent qualm,
    To smarting outrage makes us bow.

We stand besmirched! 'twere better on his isle forlorn
To leave him, from baseness far, from calm repose untorn...
Or, loud reclaiming him who myriad laurels wore,
Him Austerlitz hailed victor, him who's glory's child,
We, sword in hand, must needs, in wake of victory wild.
    His presence to our hearths restore.

Beseeming 'twere and fair!... the drum, the cannon's roar,
The bursting shell, our soldiers glowing as of yore
    From reckless battle won,
Dear France in triumph free, and England, baleful foe,
Aground her sins repenting, both her knees bent low;
'Twere only thus we might have hailed Napoleon!

No matter, he is here! Courage, noble France!
Thy shame and wrong shall end, thy wretched foe's advance;
    For firing in our hearts anew
Our wrath deluded, on the sepulchre's marble gored
We'll rise, both old and young, to whet our sturdy sword,
    Blunted at Waterloo!

Translation from Roussève, *The Negro in Louisiana,* 87–91.

Camille Thierry

Mr. Camille Thierry was regarded as one of our most outstanding Louisiana scholars. He was born in New Orleans but he spent most of his life in Paris, the center of enlightenment and culture. There he received a brilliant education and enjoyed the fresh air of liberty.[4]

Thierry was especially interested in poetry. His pieces pub-

---

[4]. Thierry's father came from Bordeaux: his mother was an octoroon. His brother in New Orleans was a wholesale liquor dealer. Tinker, *Creole City,* 265.

A Tribute to the Creole People of Color

lished in *Les Cenelles* were not his only compositions. His prolific pen, it is said, produced an entire book, which no doubt remained in France, his favorite country.

Nevertheless, the several pieces of his work that we do have sustain his reputation as a writer and scholar.[5] Thierry's style was elegant and graceful, with a natural mode of expression and a felicitous use of symbols. The poem we present here was composed in his youth; consequently it carries the imprint of the inclinations of a young man. However, this ardor of feeling is tempered by the reflections of a wisdom that restrains him from any exaggerated effusions.

Mr. Thierry was in business in New Orleans, but he did not care for that life and retired while a young man. He was well to do and, thus without financial worries, was able to give himself up entirely to his real interests. He was of average build and of distinguished appearance. We have chosen his poem, "L'Amante du Corsaire [The Corsair's Sweetheart]," to illustrate the merits of our young poet.

L'AMANTE DU CORSAIRE
[THE CORSAIR'S SWEETHEART]

To Madame * * *

Little seabird, who doubtless
    came from shores afar,
Tell me, did you not meet in your wanderings
    a trim brigantine?

Did you not, fatigued, rest a while on
    her swaying mast,
Did you not play among the ropes and her white,
    wind-filled sails?

Did you not hear the voice that is so dear
    to me—the voice of my beloved,

---

5. A volume entitled *Les Vagabonds* [*The Vagabonds*] was published in Bordeaux in 1874, the year before Thierry died. *Ibid.*, 265. Acclaimed in Europe, *Les Vagabonds* portrays three typical colored beggars who wandered the streets of New Orleans during the poet's boyhood. Rousseve, *The Negro in Louisiana*, 78, 58.

Our People and Our History

> Asking the breeze for the perfume of earth
>   to calm his longing?
> If I, like you, had wings to attempt the voyage,
>   I would forsake this place
> Like the white cloud, I would go
>   floating above these shores.
>
> To speak with him again... to say, "I love you,"
>   I would brave the ocean;
> To kiss his hair, I would go to him
>   Though storm clouds were gathering!
>
> For, you know, my love is a strange love
>   With nothing at all of earth;
> It may come from a demon or an angel...
>   I, myself, I do not know!
>
> My brothers unblushingly say I am mad
>   And come not near me;
> My sisters no longer address me...
>   I think of this with pain!
>
> In vain I tell them, "But I am your sister!"
>   Yet on their hardened hearts
> My plea makes no more impression
>   Than do wings in the air!...
>
> To whom can I tell the secret of my heart,
>   O little seabird?...
> To my mother who loved me?... No, she is gone.
>   Her soul to God! Her body to earth!
>
> Little seabird, who no doubt
>   Came from shores afar,
> Tell me, did you not meet in your wanderings
>   A brigantine?

Camille Thierry also composed the following poems: "Le Damné [The Damned]," "Le Passé [The Past]," "Toi [You]," "Adieu [Good-bye]," "Le Réveil [The Awakening]," "A Mademoiselle *** [To Miss ***]," "A Celle que J'aime [To Her Whom I Love]," "Idées [Ideas]," "L'Ombre d'Eugène B. [The Ghost of Eugene B.]," "Parle Toujours [Speak Always]," "Le Suicide [The Suicide]," "Jalousie [Jealousy]."

As it was for our poet Dalcour, France was Thierry's first love.

A Tribute to the Creole People of Color

It was there he published that small volume we would be happy to possess today. Unfortunately, through the negligence of his compatriots, the book has been lost to us. Thierry understood the apathetic disposition of his people. He realized that a man such as he could count only upon himself in the battles of life. In one of his short poems he expresses this thought:

> I heard no voice speak to me,
> Not even the voice of a mother.
> I fought alone when the thunder roared...
> I comforted myself!

Pierre Dalcour

This poet is one of the men of 1844 whom we will treat at length in another part of this book. Pierre Dalcour was born in New Orleans, but he was reared and educated in Paris. In later years he returned to New Orleans to share the life of his people, but he found the restrictions on him as a person too rigid. Like so many others, he had to return to France where he could enjoy freedom and all the advantages that science, literature, and the arts offer to spirits that nourish themselves on such things. The charms of such a hospitable society must necessarily exercise a great influence on the character, feelings, and tastes of an accomplished man like Pierre Dalcour. It was completely natural that he should return to France, for what man, accustomed from childhood to contact with civilization, could conform himself to the degradation of slavery and racial prejudice?

These unfortunate voluntary exiles like Dalcour could only dream of their mothers and feel pity for the fate of those women who had given them life, and this compassion added further to the sufferings of their unsettled souls.

It was while Dalcour was on a visit to New Orleans that he composed the selections we find in the pages of *Les Cenelles*.[6]

---

6. Pierre Dalcour contributed twelve poems to *Les Cenelles*. Edward Larocque Tinker, *Les écrits de langue française en Louisiane au XIX⁰ siècle* (Paris: Libraire Ancienne Honoré Champion, 1932), 83. To honor Dalcour, Lanusse opens and closes *Les Cenelles* with two of Dalcour's poems, "Chant d'Amour [Song of Love]" and "Desenchantement [Disenchantment]." Rousséve, *The Negro in Louisiana*, 8.

He was endowed with a ready, quick mind that made improvisation easy for him. At a moment's notice he could create a poem on any subject. The one cited here is taken from page 103 in *Les Cenelles*. Once when he was among a group of people who were playing innocent games, he was ordered by a young man to redeem his pledge by making a declaration of love to a woman of his choice. Immediately Dalcour approached a young lady who was known to be rather pious and addressed to her these lines:

> Miss,
> Apart from you there is no joy;
> You give me Faith that leads to Hope;
> To satisfy this heart of mine,
> Would you, in Charity, give me a kiss?

The subject, as one sees, revolves around the three theological virtues: Faith, Hope, and Charity, so tenderly rendered into verse by Millevoye. We know also that Dalcour was held in high regard and esteem by his friends and his colleagues. Armand Lanusse and Camille Thierry addressed to him several pieces of poetry and gave to him other testimonials of their appreciation.

Dalcour, Thierry, and Valcour were surrounded by men of letters and by some of the leading intellectuals of Europe. Among these were Hugo, Dumas, and other celebrities who made the past century illustrious.

Pierre Dalcour has left us the following selections: "Chant d'Amour [Song of Love]," "Un An d'Absence [A Year of Absence]," "A Une Inconstante [To an Unfaithful Woman]," "Le Songe [The Dream]," "Le Maudit [The Damned One]," "Au Bord du Lac [On the Shore of the Lake]," "La Foi, L'Espérance et la Charité [Faith, Hope and Charity]," "Acrostiche [An Acrostic]," "Les Aveux [Confessions]," "Caractère [Character]," "Vers Ecrits sur L'Album [Verses Written in an Album]," "Heure de Désenchantement [Hour of Disenchantment]."

Pierre Dalcour, Armand Lanusse, and Camille Thierry contributed more than any other writers to *Les Cenelles*, and their writings surpassed all others (if we except Séjour and Questy).

A Tribute to the Creole People of Color

From among the various works of Dalcour, we have chosen to present here his "Chant d'Amour [Song of Love]." It is a model of mixed verse, filled with imagery, lively action, loving and graceful lines. The selection reveals the true character of the poet, with his many resources of style, sensitivity, and creative ability. He is precise in his comparisons, fluent and picturesque in his phrasing and composition. We may say of Dalcour what Boileau wrote of Molière: "Never does he bungle his choice of words."

CHANT D'AMOUR
[SONG OF LOVE]

Aid me, O my lyre, to praise the
    beauty I adore!
Bring to her on the wings of the breeze
    your sweetest tones.

From the wave that expires upon the shore,
    from the birds in the air,
From the evening zephyr caressing the trees,
    borrow your melodies.

Borrow from the night its thousand harmonies,
    strange but sweet,
That seem to the soul an angelic choir
    singing in the skies.

Should my lips never dare vow to her
    my ardent love,
Tell her today, O my lyre, the mystery,
    this secret of my heart.

May your beautiful melodies linger on
    receding slowly,
Like a faraway concert, like a symphony
    dying out in a distant echo!...

* * *

May a breeze so light,
When day has fled
Into the mystery of night,
Bring to her, my beloved,
This song of love.

Our People and Our History

As the shades of night gather
In an immense cloud,
To cover the earth in silence;
When all under heaven is in repose,
Hour of sweet reverie,
At times her cherished face
Seems present to me!

I see her form so like a sylph,
With forehead pure, and candid grace;
Her lips of coral—moist—
Her eyes so black and filled with languor;
I feel a living spark
Escaping from her glance,
Only to embrace my heart!

I think, too, in my ecstasy
I hear her voice that sighs
More gently than the wind
That plays among the branches,
And is sweeter than the murmur
Of the clear stream whose water pure,
Winds slowly among the reeds.

When a gentle breeze
Caresses the perfumed flower
And lifts itself up inebriated
At evening time toward the vaulted canopy of heaven,
I think that I am inhaling
The fragrant breath of my beloved
In these delightful perfumes.

But, alas! Soon this mirage
Which reflects her image
Takes flight as a wispy cloud
When chased by the impetuous wind!
Or as, with the breaking of dawn,
One sees the shadows soon disappearing
In the first luminous rays of the sun.

In vain, I cry out to myself:
Come back, O sweet beloved dream
Shadow, deceptive and yet dear;
Come back at least one last time!
Alas, as my voice calls to her,

A Tribute to the Creole People of Color

I hear but a faithful echo
That responds to my call from afar!...

Revive yourself, O my lyre!—an expiring lamp
Gives one last flicker before it dies;
Strike one last song from your vibrant chords
To tell of the agony of my impassioned heart!

Whether the day-star illumes both the earth and the sky
With its brilliance,
Or the dark mystery of night
Falls like a veil, silently;

Maiden, it is you always who fills my thoughts,
Who makes my heart to throb,
Who restores hope to my crushed soul,
Weakened under the burden of sorrow.

It is you who appear at night in my dreams,
O' my beautiful one!
It is for you I seek
At dawn—
On awakening!

Often I seem to see a shadowy form
Floating around me,
A shadow the light of day cannot dispel;
It is you—it is always you!

O deceiver, O vain shadow,
Can a dream bring us happiness?...
Oft for the dreamer of happiness
The awakening is but frightful!

Come, O come! Release me from this sorrow
Which now engulfs me,
Come, for my only happiness on this earth
Is to be loved!

For love, only the love of a maiden adored
Can console the heart burdened with sorrow;
It is a fresh oasis, it is the sacred manna,
It is the source of pure water in the midst of a desert!

B. Valcour

B. Valcour was born in New Orleans. If we should judge by the date of his writings, he would rank among the oldest contribu-

Our People and Our History

tors to *Les Cenelles*.[7] He was educated in France under the direction of good teachers, as he himself states in his "Letter to Constant Lépouzé," the poet. He knew Latin and Greek. Valcour appeals to us because of his frankness and because of the classical tone which he maintains in his elegant, polished verse. He does not hesitate to tell us that he is a poet and that he is familiar with the works of Horace and Vergil. He writes with assurance: he states that he knows the rules of poetic art, and they support his claims by giving us the most harmonious and well-ordered Alexandrine lines. Valcour occasionally employs allegory in his poetry, but this ruse is attributed more to caprice than to fault. He chose to use in his compositions the *rimes plates*, the *rimes croisées*, and the regular stanza. However, he has written one or two selections that have mixed versification. But in all his poetry, he conforms scrupulously to the rules of poetic art. His versification flows easily, and his rhymes, without being rich, are most pleasing to the ear. They never lack harmony.

The selection that follows, taken from *Les Cenelles*, was composed in 1828. We do not know Mr. Valcour's age when he wrote this poem, but he must have been still a youth, because he addressed the lines to his teacher.

EPITRE À CONSTANT LÉPOUZÉ EN RECEVANT
UN VOLUME DE SES POÉSIES
[LETTER TO CONSTANT LÉPOUZÉ ON RECEIVING
A VOLUME OF HIS POETRY]

I have not forgotten, despite my long silence,
That as a child I was submissive to your rule:

7. The dates of Valcour's birth and death are unknown. He was probably born about 1800, as the letter to his teacher, Lépouzé, published in *Les Cenelles*, is dated 1828. Edward Maceo Coleman, *Creole Voices: Poems in French by Free Men of Color* (Washington, D.C.: The Associated Publishers, 1945), 13. No trace can be found of Valcour's first name. In *Les Cenelles*, to which he contributed eleven poems, he signs himself Valcour B +++. "B. Valcour introduces lines by Lamartine as mottoes, refers to his Elvire, and publishes one of his own poems as an imitation of Beranger.... Many of the themes [of poems featured in *Les Cenelles*] are those already treated by French Romanticists. There may, too, have been some influence from their classical predecessors that kept these Louisiana writers from localizing their poems more than they do...." *Ibid.*, vi.

A Tribute to the Creole People of Color

I cherish the remembrance of all your kindness,
And I have kept all your precepts in my heart.

It is to you I owe my love of poetry;
You instructed me in its metrical rhyme;
My muse still untried, sensitive and discreet,
Sings for you her first song.

May my muse never be effaced by time!
The key to the language of the gods, you gave me;
The rhythmic beat of Horace you taught me,
With the harmony of Vergil you endowed me!

A mere ambitious teacher you were not,
Exchanging his talents for a weight of gold,
Whose pen of steel never wrote except to say,
"I have received," at the end of the month.

No one ever saw you, Professor Gros-Jean,
Borrow your knowledge from Constant Letellier;
Nor make of us an obscure monopoly—
Selling the desks as well as the students!

No, we have not seen you entering marking in the journal
An *A* bulging with pride or a *Z* for talkative mischief,
Nor did you extend indiscreet praise to a friend
Or false eulogy of an illegitimate Maecenas!

O Artist, praise be unto you! Take glory as a poet!
You, bold rival of Lavan, of Daru,
Through you, Louisiana enjoys a festival,
On the shores of her great river, a Horace has appeared.

Why do you not sit in the Coliseum,
And question about the remains of Poestum
Or relive in a dream, abandoned Ferrara,
Seek the treasurers of Pompeii, and those of Herculaneum?

I tell myself: Son, it is time to acknowledge
The modest rhetorician, to give the praise that's his;
I have but one word for you O teacher: It is Thanks.
From my mouth it comes forth, but my heart really says it!

All that we can add in reflection is that the feelings expressed in the preceding verses demonstrate in a singularly clear manner everything good or bad in the artistic influence of contact. From the Lépouzés come Valcours. Other poems written by

Valcour are: "L'Heureux Pèlerin [The Happy Pilgrim]," "A Malvina [To Malvina]," "A Hermina [To Hermina]," "Le 11 mars, 1835 [March 11, 1835]," "L'Ouvrier Louisianais, [A Louisiana Laborer]," "A Mon Ami [To My Friend]," "Mon Rêve [My Dream]," "Son Chapeau et Son Châle [Her Hat and her Shawl]," "A Mademoiselle Célina [To Miss Celine]," "A Mademoiselle C. [To Miss C.]."

Jean Boise

Jean Boise had a reputation as an excellent author, but his mind became clouded during the period of his life when he was offering the greatest promise of literary ability. His friends regretted this because of his fine character and his excellent talents. Boise's insanity resulted from an illness that terminated his life too soon to fulfill the hopes of his contemporaries. The last stanza of the selection we cite below reveals him as Lamartine would describe him, "a soul sad, even unto his death." [8]

L'AMANT DÉDAIGNE
[THE SCORNED LOVER]

Perfidious Love, rebellious Divinity,
You who rule mortals and gods,
Why must your cruel arrow
Strike the breast of a despised mortal?
I who desired in the springtime of youth
To rejoice amid pleasures in peace,
You detain me in my fleeting course;
Is your heart jealous, perhaps, of my happiness?

[Life has] no more allurements,
No more charm,
All is sad to my eyes;
You frighten and alarm me,
Day itself is odious.
My limbs are weak, feeble...
What shall I become?

8. Jean Boise was a native of New Orleans, but the exact dates of his birth and death are unknown. He is noted especially for his poem, "The Scorned Lover," published in *Les Cenelles. Ibid.*, xxv.

A Tribute to the Creole People of Color

My eyes are dull,
Alas! Must I die?

Tell me, my sweet friend,
Tell me what have I done to you?
Without you, I hate life,
Without you, all displeases me.
You still say nothing...
What shall I become?
Vainly I implore you!
Alas! I am going to die!

Tell me, what is my crime?
May I not know?
Shall I be the victim
Of cruel despair?
You keep silent...
What shall I become?...
Pronounce my sentence;
Tell me, must I die?

It is finished, I succumb
To my sinister lot;
On my forehead, already falls
The veil of death.
Good-bye, cruel friend,
My torments are over,
I quit this life.
Good-bye, I am going to die!

[?] *Bowers*

Although we have no information on the life, character, or merit of Mr. Bowers, we think it proper and wise to publish the selection he has left us. The subject is eloquent, the style fluent and well sustained. Mr. Bowers was a contributor to *Les Cenelles*. This fact, as well as his poetry, is appreciated. It is fitting, therefore, that he be featured in this book.[9]

---

9. Bowers was a New Orleanian. There is no other identification for him, except this last name given by Desdunes. Even this name is often abbreviated to a pen name, such as Bo...rs, Bo...as, B...s. Bowers also published his "L'Orphelin des Tombeaux" in *La Lorgnette* and his "Vision" in *Le Dimanche* in 1802. *Ibid.*, xxiii.

Our People and Our History

L'ORPHELIN DES TOMBEAUX
[THE ORPHAN AMONG THE TOMBS]

I

Not long ago an orphan with a plaintive voice
Poured out his sorrows to a field sown with crosses;
He sang, and the birds hidden in the foliage,
Seemed to still their song, to listen to him;
He sang, and the breezes ceased blowing,
The murmur of the waters sighed sadly;
He sang, and my heart softened, even to tears,
And melted at the recital;
He sang, and now and then
His funeral songs seemed suddenly to send a chill through me!

II

When evening came, pensive and alone,
Gazing sadly at the ground
I began to cry, thinking of him
Who had once said to me: "I am your support;
I will be the consolation of your deplorable state;
The world despises you; alas! tell me, are you guilty?
If you suffer misfortunes here below,
If everywhere adversity accompanies you, tell me.
No, no, you are not guilty; I weep over your fate.
Child, do you accept the shelter of my poor home?
Do you wish to live with me, unfortunate one?
I will henceforth be your adopted parent,
I will make your life pleasant; Alas! you are to be pitied.
Child, in my dwelling you will have nothing to fear;
Stormy weather, I would keep from your life,
Because you will be my son forever;
I will dispel all your troubles, yes, in my old house
Oh, come rest yourself, melancholy child."
In ending this talk, taking me by the hand;
To his cheerful, pleasing home he led me at once;
He called me his son; I said to him: my father.
A child, yet he showed me a prosperous future.
Already I was happy, only at times
 The sad memory of a touching voice came to break
The charm of my gaiety
And suddenly would force me to weep again;
But when I saw him—this generous friend,
Sleeping the sleep of death,

A Tribute to the Creole People of Color

I checked my tears in his presence,
And suddenly was soothed with an unexpected joy;
For he knew always what consoling words to say,
Words which assuaged the sorrow and the tears,
Words like honey, so sweet and so beautiful,
That they allayed my pains so rebellious!
So he is dead, this generous Father!...
At his death I burst into anguished sobs!
For, I still remember his last sigh:
It was in the month of March, at the break of dawn...
I had gone to visit the tomb of my sister,
When, all of a sudden, I heard a plaintive, tender voice,
Murmuring a name I could not understand.
I listened... That voice, which made me sigh,
Murmured: "Your Father is dying now, Child,
Do you not hear? This is his voice that is calling you.
Come and place your hand on his bed of suffering;
Come, present your lips to kiss him good-bye;
On his bed of pain, remember him to God!"
Seated on the edge of the bed, I listened,
Turning pale, I listened to those last words,
Which escaped slowly from his mouth:
"It is finished, O my son; I leave you forever;
At my abandoned tomb you will henceforth pray!...
Each day and you will come at the break of dawn,
Child, to mourn there, to kneel again...
Let me press your hand... It is over... I die."
And his voice faded away in tears,
Alas, he is no more! On his cold mausoleum
I breathe forth sometime my sad desolation.
Each morning of my days it is thus; this is my lot,
Banished from the entire world, I weep over death!
Bewildered, sorrowful in this dark cemetery,
I contemplate the resting place of my entire family;
I am alone, always alone in this garden of tombs,
Where the weeping willow tree waves its branches,
Where often tired, I rest in the shade
Of an ancient cypress tree... there a sad dreamer,
In the shade of an angel's wings, an angel
Of fifteen years crowned with jasmines;
I imagine sometimes I am pressing her pulsating hands
I dream of holding her in my arms, this modest virgin,
Inebriated by a look from her weeping eyes!

But, suddenly, I awake, murmuring these words:
Alas! it is only a dream in the middle of the tombs!
Ah, the very remembrance of you, angel so kind,
Brings an inexpressible charm to my woes.
But soon, I feel I am going to sleep at last,
With a sleep, alas, that has no end!
Then, Anastasia, in gazing upon my tomb,
May a tear of love moisten your cheek!
May you note the meaning of these words:
"He lived and died in the midst of the tombs."

III

The echo repeated again his orphan cry;
And with two arms crossed on his youthful breast,
He lay asleep while dreaming of the skies;
The torch in flaming light now fell upon his hair;
And when the bird sang out its reveille of dawn,
In that same posture he was sleeping still:
Yes, but in the sleep of death whose mournful stamp
Imprints upon our hearts eternal regret!...

Louis Boise

Louis Boise was the brother of Jean Boise. We have heard older people say that Louis Boise did not learn to read until he was twenty years old.[10] If that is true, he is worthy of being counted among our prodigies, because a man of ordinary intelligence would not be able to begin so late and succeed so well in the composition of verse such as that quoted below. The task was enormous, but the success was marvelous!

AU PRINTEMPS
[TO SPRING]

Sweet Spring, come unto waiting Nature; yield
Thy treasures and allure both bright and fair.
To hail thee, troubadours, in verdant field,
In song shall praises of thy blessings bear.

---

10. Louis Boise was born and reared, like his brother Jean, in New Orleans, which city neither man ever left. *Ibid.*, xxv. Louis was a tailor and lived at 72 Craps, now Burgundy, Street. *Cohen's New Orleans Directory, 1852* (New Orleans: Office of the *Daily Delta*, 1852), 30. His poem "Springtime" is published in *Les Cenelles.*

A Tribute to the Creole People of Color

By beds of myrtles and of roses gay,
Thou'lt hear me, by thy sweet return made glad,
To my dear Cloé tender whisperings say;
Thou'lt find me in love's brightest raiment clad.

Glad lovers all, in their new songs of mirth,
'Neath rooftrees fresh and green thy name shall praise;
In leafy groves the faithful birds of earth
Shall join to warble blithsome roundelays.

Then haste thee, come, for Nature, steeped in hoar,
Shares wretched lot of Winter sombre, sear;
She sighs, thy gladsome presence doth implore;
She weeps... her anguished voice canst thou not hear?

Translation by Charles B. Roussève, May, 1935.

Chapter IV
The Collaborators of *Les Cenelles* (Continuation) ∽ Biographical Sketches

Michel St. Pierre

Mr. Michel St. Pierre was a poet and a fencing master.[1] His poetry is natural and graceful: all of his poems are written in a flowing style, filled with charm. He was of an affectionate nature and this quality is reflected in his verse. The poem entitled "Le Changement [The Change]" serves well to introduce St. Pierre and to illustrate his good nature and disposition. He addressed it to a girl he loved at a moment when he decided to abandon bachelorhood for married life. For some curious reason, the song became very popular with children, who learned it quickly and sang it with much pleasure.

Because of his courage and firm determined will, he was nicknamed "The Creole Bayard."[2] Armand Lanusse who preached the discourse at his funeral spoke of St. Pierre as a remarkably brave man.

St. Pierre was born in New Orleans into a large and respectable family whose children were all highly educated. All were devout Catholics from their early childhood. St. Pierre's religious feelings manifest themselves often in his writings. At one

---

1. St. Pierre was born in the early 1800's and lived in the city of his birth until he died, about 1865. Little is known of his early life. He contributed to *L'Album Littéraire* and wrote "Le Changement [The Change]" for *Les Cenelles*. Edward Maceo Coleman, *Creole Voices: Poems in French by Free Men of Color* (Washington, D.C.: The Associated Publishers, 1945), xiii. New Orleans city directories for 1841 to 1853 list his address as Ursuline Street, between Villere and Robertson.

2. The "Bayard" is Chevalier Pierre du Terrail Bayard (1473–1524), the famous French captain who distinguished himself in the Italian wars of Charles VIII, Louis XII, and Francis I. He came to be known as the "knight without fear and without reproach." Paul Harvey and Janet Heseltine(eds.), *The Oxford Companion to French Literature* (Oxford: Clarendon Press, 1959), 54.

A Tribute to the Creole People of Color

time in his life, he contemplated suicide, but on the advice of a friend, he overcame this desire to take his life by recalling the beliefs of his faith, which only folly can undermine.[3]

LE CHANGEMENT
[THE CHANGE]

In a sweet indifference
I lived, peaceful and content;
To me love seemed without strength:
Therefore, I often affronted it;
But, the sweet pleasures of my life,
Alas, they couldn't last always,
Since your beautiful eyes, Amélie,
Have interrupted the course.

Nevertheless, if I could please you,
If you would smile at my vows,
I will make a sincere confession to you,
You would render me more than happiness;
For the happiness that I breathe
When I find myself beside you,
Is a happiness... a sweet delight,
Of whom a thousand lovers would be jealous!

On your pretty face
One sees goodness, candor,
Innocence and modesty,
And all that makes a good heart.
When in a full look of fire,
Sometimes, I interrogate your eyes
The hope seems to tell my soul
That you share my fire.

Translation from Coleman, *Creole Voices*, 83–84.

Other selections of Michel St. Pierre are: "La Jeune Fille Mourante [The Young Girl Dying]," "A Une Demoiselle [To a Young Lady]," "Deux Ans Après [Two Years Later]," "Coup-

---

3. This friend was Auguste Populus of New Orleans, to whom St. Pierre wrote a "thank you" poem entitled "Deux Ans Après [Two Years Later]" and addressed it, "To my friend, A. Populus." Coleman, *Creole Voices*, 83–84. The poem appears in *Les Cenelles*, 138; it is translated in Coleman, *Creole Voices*, 86–87.

lets [Couplets]," "Tu M'as Dit [You Told Me]," "Je t'Aime [I Love You]."

Numa Lanusse

A graseful style, an elegant form, and a natural gaiety: such are the qualities that distinguish Numa Lanusse's "Couplets." These verses testify that the author possessed a beautiful poetic talent that would undoubtedly have developed with his age, had death not surprised him prematurely. He has numerous admirers. Mr. Lanusse died at the age of twenty-six, as a result of a fall from a horse.

COUPLETS
CHANTES A LA NOCE D'UN AMI
[SONGS AT THE WEDDING OF A FRIEND]

(Sung to the melody of: I Hear in the Distance the Bow of Love.)

O happy lovers, you of Cythère
Who launch on your voyage uncertain,
May a sweet wind and a favorable sea
Conduct you with love to your destiny;
May no sinister clouds
Your sweet sojourn disturb;
Sail on, O friends, without any fear of storms,
Our wishes of love will lead you to port.

The ship bounds forward and the winds are propitious,
A sweet hope caresses your tender, young hearts;
Love follows and crowns you with flowers
To keep away tempests, shipwrecks and floods;
To guard you—we pray in common accord;
Sail on, O friends, with no fear of storms,
Our wishes of love will lead you to port.

A stealthy wind rises, your sails to invade
Your voyage is slackened in flight;
The sky is in darkness and waves froth in anger,
But, no... hope still lifts you,
And truth dissipates clouds;
The air now is cleansed, your barque moves forward.
Sail on, O friends, with no fear of storms,
Our wishes of love will lead you to port.

A Tribute to the Creole People of Color

> Already the shoreline you're able to see,
> There fortune and happiness await you;
> Love slowly but surely gives way to friendship,
> And this, O dear lovers, will be your support.
> You smile, it is true, when prophecies say
> That beautiful children will come to you soon.
> Sail on, O friends, with no fear of storms,
> Their concern, their cares, will lead you to port!

Mr. Numa Lanusse composed another poem, "Justification," which was published in *Les Cenelles*. It was worthy of the reputation of the author. It seems he was accused by a young girl of having written some couplets against her. The poem "Justification" was written in denial of this charge. We regret we cannot, for lack of space, reproduce the entire work, but we believe we should give the following excerpt, which we have often heard quoted by our people—ignorant, perhaps, of the true source of the lines:

> Do not listen to what people say,
> Because too often this destroys happiness.

There is more poetry in these two lines than a mere outsider thinks. Only the Creole can well appreciate the philosophy of their meaning.

Desormes Dauphin

The selection that follows is an expression of despair. One will notice that all of our poets put emotion into their compositions. Whether the subject is sad or gay, simple or majestic, the expression, the manner in which they express their ideas never lacks the effect of art enhanced by strong, deep sentiment. In these lines of Dauphin all is mournful and somber. The poet seems to have conceived them while in a morbid state of mind, but as to the clarity of thought, as well as the purity of the language, nothing in these selected poems surpasses the excellence of the strophe here produced.

Our People and Our History

ADIEUX
[GOOD-BYES]

Dearest one, why have you
So soon dispelled the transports of my love?
Do you remember the days when you were so enamored
And you promised me a happiness without regret?
Adieu, good-bye, pardon if my faithful heart
Cannot detach itself from you;
I am going to pay today with my life
For the happy day when I received your trust.

> Good-bye, from the celestial vault of heaven,
> I will watch over your destiny;
> There will end the unhappiness of life,
> Which already approaches its end;

When tormented by a secret pain,
Your fickle heart will recognize the sorrow.
Come, pray to God at my tomb, please
For there you will be reborn to happiness.
And the Eternal One hearing your prayer,
In memory of our past love,
Will place a flower on the marble tomb
Which will cover my dried remains;

> Good-bye from the celestial vault of heaven,
> I will watch over your destiny;
> There will end the unhappiness of life,
> Which already approaches its end.

Nelson Desbrosses

Nelson Desbrosses was a native of New Orleans.[4] Eminently respectable and popular among his confreres, like most of them he too received his education in private schools from conscientious teachers. Growing up, he was mindful of the society and times in which he lived and he cultivated the Muses. He frequented the company of the poets of his day, and it is thus that we find his verse in *Les Cenelles*.

4. There is no record of his birth or death dates. He was a cigar maker who lived and died in New Orleans. Edward Larocque Tinker, *Les écrits de langue française en Louisiane au XIXe siècle* (Paris: Libraire Ancienne Honoré Champion, 1932), 134.

A Tribute to the Creole People of Color

Desbrosses visited Haiti and spent several years there, but it is in Louisiana that he made his career. He was not only known as a poet, but even more as a virtuous man. Gifted by nature with certain peculiar aptitudes, he seriously undertook to develop them. He became a friend of the famous Valmour, who instructed him and from whom he received advice needed to obtain the powers he desired in "the laying on of hands and in the transmission of spiritual messages." In time he became a master at his useful art, as many people who are indebted to him can attest.

LE RETOUR AU VILLAGE AUX PERLES*
[THE RETURN TO THE VILLAGE OF PEARLS]

Romance
She frolics in these places filled with charms,
Everything tells me this, yes, my heart senses it well.
Joyous abode, you banish my tears,
God of Love, what happiness is mine!
O flowering tree, testimony of our love,
I see you again and this is real truth.
Dear little stream, it is to you that my soul
Wishes on this day to confide its joy.
But there she is! How beautiful!
Ah! What beauty! What feminine charms!
She smiles... Ah! how beautiful she is!
Charming Emma, I fly to you!

March, 1828

*Au. note.—A nickname given by the author of this romance and by Numa Lanusse to the Bayou Road because of the large number of beautiful young girls who lived in the neighborhood of the Clark family home.

One sees with what care and concern our poets wrote of the young beauties of their time. "The Village of Pearls" is undoubtedly the place that inspired Armand Lanusse when, in his introduction to *Les Cenelles*, he alluded to "the charming Louisianians whose beauty, grace, and amiability will live on without doubt in all their marvelous purity in those who will come after them." Desbrosses completed his task well. How natural is his exclamation, "But there she is! How beautiful!" We are happy to say we still have with us a good number of those pearls.

F. Liotau

F. Liotau has left us a number of very fine poems. The one cited here, entitled "An Impression," is one of his most successful.[5] In his lines the author expresses his respect for the Catholic religion and his hopes for the union of Christian hearts. Liotau is conscious of his style in all his compositions, be they humorous or serious.[6] He is witty and imaginative. He never shows lack of feeling in his poetry, and he concludes each composition with no indication of having exhausted his effort. Other poems by Liotau are: "Un An Après [One Year Later]," "Eline [Elaine]," "Mon Vieux Chapeau [My Old Hat]," "A Ida [To Ida]," "Couplets Chantés à Une Noce [Couplets Sung at a Wedding]," "A Un Ami Qui m'Accusait de Plagiat [To a Friend Who Accused Me of Plagiarism]," "Un Condamné à Mort [One Condemned to Death]."

UNE IMPRESSION
[AN IMPRESSION]

St. Louis Church, aged temple, shrine,
You now stand there solitary, deserted!
Those who once were charged with your care,
In scorn today have left the holy tabernacle;
They have elsewhere led their Christian flock
To worship until each one repents of his error;
Alas, on your flagstones, we will never see again
The children of Jesus kneeling,
Those who with attentive ear and timorous soul,
Listened to the sacred words of their pastors.
From the precious precincts of your sanctuary;
No longer will the perfumed incense rise up into the sky!...

5. The poem "Une Impression" is one of eight selections by Liotau in *Les Cenelles*, 162.
6. Little is known of Liotau's life except that he was born in New Orleans and died there in 1847. He wrote for *L'Album Littéraire* and for *Les Cenelles*. Tinker, *Les écrits de langue française*, 292.

A Tribute to the Creole People of Color

Your beautiful altars, your ancient statues,
Your crosses, vestments, and holy relics,
Alas, they will rest in complete oblivion
Which already has them within its folds!...
O divine temple, you the final home,
Of our beloved dead whom people still mourn,
And who, perhaps also resenting your wrongs,
Do groan as we do from the depths of their graves;
You who saw me as a child within your walls,
Receive on my forehead the sign of baptism;
Alas, have I lived to see you today,
Abandoned, deserted, empty, perhaps, forever!...
August and venerable sanctuary where every soul rejoiced
As the choir sang the sacred liturgy,
Will you remain always deprived of your honors?
Since never in vain do we pray to Our Lord,
Christians, let us unite—for our loving God
Poured out His blood for us on Calvary;
Let us hope that soon He, alone the all-powerful and strong,
On hearing our plea will change our lot;
Let us pray if we will that His mercy
Will wipe out among us all hatred and discord.
Has not this hope previously, in drying our tears,
Brought balm to our sorrowing hearts?
Have we not witnessed before the people of Orleans,
Comfortably gathered here for the great feast day;*
It was then that true happiness shown in their eyes,
As all was forgotten on this occasion of joy!
Christians, one more effort will tip the balance
Surely toward peace; let us have confidence;
And we will see again as in the past,
That our people each day will come once more to this abandoned sanctuary!...

*Au. note—St. Barbara, patroness of artillerymen.

Auguste Populus

"A Mon Ami P. [To My Friend P.]," "Acrostiche [Acrostic]," and "Reponse à Mon Ami Michel St. Pierre [An Answer to My Friend, Michel St. Pierre]" are the works carrying the name of this poet. Mr. Auguste Populus was a stonemason. Despite his being ill with tuberculosis, his devotion to study and his love for things intellectual won for him the esteem and the admiration of his contemporaries. He died when he was scarcely forty-six years old. He was a native of New Orleans and a close friend of Michel St. Pierre.[7] When St. Pierre contemplated suicide in a moment of despair, Populus dissuaded his friend from this act. The selection we quote here was the response to a letter from St. Pierre in which he expressed his gratitude to the poet for calling him back to reason or, as he says, "to the virtues." This circumstance gives a solemnity to the work, and it also makes its sublime inspiration evident.

REPONSE A MON AMI MICHEL ST-PIERRE
[ANSWER TO MY FRIEND MICHEL ST. PIERRE]

When lightning's ceased, and heaven more beauteous then
Anew her robe of purest azure dons;
When, a smile with hope, the orb that lights our way
Throws far his veil, and forth sends radiance bright;
To hail the blest return of dawning day,
The blithesome nightingale sings loud his song:
Thus, since thy muse today awakes anew,
And charming sounds have reached my raptured ear,
To me 'tis sweet to think thy courage bold
Has conquered baleful wrath of envious Fate.
Now qualms no more, nor silence gloomy, cold,
May happiness, dear friend, succeed thy woe.
Dash from thy heart the gloom-infested past,
That thou by valiant striving could'st redeem;
Lo in thy songs extol this victory great;
Your return to the virtues crowns thee with glory.[8]

Translation by Charles B. Roussève, May, 1935.

Nicol Riquet

Nicol Riquet was a wealthy cigar maker who lived in New Or-

7. Auguste Populus' birth and death dates are not known. In *Les Cenelles*, to which he contributed three poems, including the one reproduced herein, he signs only his initials, A. P. Populus was associated with the Louisiana state treasurer after the Civil War. Tinker, *Les écrits de langue française*, 378.

8. Auguste Populus wrote these verses in answer to the poem addressed to him by St. Pierre. The poem appears in *Les Cenelles*, 140.

A Tribute to the Creole People of Color

leans all his life. He composed easily and is said to have assisted the development of several would-be writers of his day. A number of romantic poems, which were never printed but which the youth of his day loved to sing, are among his compositions. His "Rondeau Redouble [Double Round]" has the distinction of being the only composition of this nature published in *Les Cenelles* [p. 75]. Because of its title, it attracts immediate interest. A naïve piece of work, it is addressed to the god Bacchus.

RONDEAU REDOUBLE
[DOUBLE ROUND]

To Free Friends

Free Friends ask for a rondo.
Come on, my Muse, we must create a marvel!
Let us not write, however, for mere water,
For they will pay us good old wine by the bottle.

To get you, O sweet juice of the vine!...
I must compose a new kind of rhyme,
And I must not sleep until I do:
For Free Friends deserve a rondo.

Of wine, Bacchus promises a cask;
While Love offers a basket of flowers;
But I prefer the gift of good wine.
Come on, my Muse, we must create a marvel.

At night, I spend hours writing,
And at day my verses all fall into water!
Oh, well, from now on, O Muse, I tell you,
In truth, we shall not write for water.

From the depths of my heart, I feel pouring
A new poem of unparalleled rhyme;
Let us go, O Muse, to create a wonder:
They will pay us with a bottle of old wine!

Alas, as to those who will blame us
We will pass them and give a quick bow;
To their speeches we will listen quite well,
But as rhymesters we will not excel...

By Free Friends

Our People and Our History

Manuel Sylva

Manuel Sylva, it is said, was a man of true modesty but of exceptional talent. He wrote only two poems for *Les Cenelles*, one entitled "Le Rêve [The Dream]"; the other, "Soudain [Suddenly]," which we quote herein. Sylva was of Spanish descent, as he indicates in his *Literary Essay*:

> To the songs of a thousand birds, to those of the nightingale,
> I dared to mingle my voice in a Spanish melody.
> Ah, I sang about Adèle and to my mother dear,
> I sang about all the delights of a beautiful country.

The idea of slavery weighed heavily on Sylva's sensitive nature. He dreamed of the charms of a country he called his own, and one which was still the home of his beloved parents.

SOUDAIN
[SUDDENLY]

To be sung to the melody of: I Saw Everywhere in My Wanderings

I renounce you, somber Lyre,
Since you lose your sweet accents,
And sing only of delirium
That holds fast to my senses.
Your sounds they but rekindle the flame,
That my heart feeds on in vain.
Ah, for the repose of my soul,
Please, O dreary Lyre, flee quickly!

And if, O Lyre, you do not return her
To my passionate heart,
I shall see her faithful image
In this little flower, the pink, that she gave me.
This flower that, even though fading,
Will ever remain on my breast...
From this worldly and profane exile
Will you flee suddenly, O sad little flower!

And so I shall forget her forever,
And go to enjoy a sweet rest!
No longer will I think of Aurelia,
But rather just memories of sorrow

A Tribute to the Creole People of Color

And tears shed for one so unfaithful
Will flow not again on tomorrow...
Yet when I do try to forget her,
My heart just suddenly refuses!

Already my madness has ceased,
O Lyre, little flower, come back.
And go away, ugly jealousy,
For Aurelia has again sought my trust,
In love all feelings are subtle,
There's pleasure, and sadness, and joy,
At a word, one gives in unguarded,
And a look does one suddenly disarm!

Victor Ernest Rillieux

Victor Ernest Rillieux was born in New Orleans [1845; died there December 5, 1898]. He descended from a family whose many members were noted for their special talents and for their valuable services to their people. As Joanni [Questy] said of William Stephens, "He died before his time." He was but fifty-three years old, comparatively young, especially for one of his potential worth.

He was poor, but never did he in any way reveal the suffering he endured because of this.[9] He divided his time between caring for his small business and writing poetry.

Rillieux was prolific in his production and wrote more than any other Louisianian. Unfortunately, only a few of his compositions remain to us. These are songs, odes and satires, and translations from the Spanish, whose merits have been recognized and praised. We have chosen to publish one of his romantic poems, which was set to music by one of our very celebrated composers, who also has left this life.

Rillieux was another Gilbert, whom he resembled both in talent and in misfortune.[10]

---

9. Rillieux was also blind. His brother was Norbert Rillieux, the inventor of sugar refining equipment. Edward Larocque Tinker, *Creole City: Its Past and Its People* (New York: Longmans, Green, 1953), 394. Norbert Rillieux is discussed in Chapter VI of this volume.

10. This is a reference to William Schwenck Gilbert of Gilbert and Sullivan.

Our People and Our History

LE TIMIDE
[THE TIMID ONE]
(MUSIC OF L.D.)

Each day I see her, charming, gracious
In the midst of flowers, under the orange blossoms;
But when the harmonious notes of her sweet song
Come to revive the fires of my tender heart,
Why, being timid, am I never in my extreme intoxication
Able to tell her I love her?

> Sing always,
> O my loves!
> Sing, sing always.

Ravished, burning with love at her side, I admire
Her graces, her beauty, her enchanting look.
Still, when from her lips there comes a sweet smile,
As a reflection of heaven comes to embace my heart,
Why, timid and weak, even in my ecstacy,
I dare not to say, alas, to this goddess whom I love

> Smile always,
> O my loves!
> Smile, smile always.

At evening in her hammock, I love to see her dream,
Oh, when she murmurs in a loving whisper
A name, a sweet, loving avowal, a pledge
In which my soul rejoices,
I listen with love as though it were a song from heaven,
Why, believing, doubting, at this moment supreme,
I cannot, oh! my God, say to this angel whom I love:

> Dream always,
> O my loves!
> Dream, dream, always.

Chapter V
Beaumont and the Creole Song ~ The Toucoutou Affair ~ Poets and Journalists

BEAUMONT AND THE CREOLE SONG

Joe [Joseph] Beaumont was born in New Orleans in 1820 and died in that city in 1872, having spent his entire life there. His even temperament and kindly attitude toward all his fellow men won for him in return their highest esteem and love. As a poet he was ingenious and natural. He composed attractive verse and never failed to impart the truth in his writings. One observes these qualities above all in his Creole songs, which always reveal a depth of thought and teach a moral based on life as it is. He was a Creole poet of distinct merit.

THE TOUCOUTOU AFFAIR[1]

Beaumont showed his special talent as a Creole song writer on the occasion of a lawsuit between two well-known families of color, a lawsuit that took place in our city a short time before the Civil War. The dispute resulted from a quarrel among some children on the street. One of the children called another a Negro. A fight ensued that created quite a disturbance, so the defense claimed.

The person attacked, rightfully sought to justify her claim that she was of the Caucasian race, that she was *white*, as the expression was then used. The prosecution proved that she was of African descent, and so she was recognized by the state supreme court.

---

1. The Toucoutou Affair refers to a well-known lawsuit that took place in New Orleans shortly before the Civil War. It became the subject of Beaumont's songs and, later, of Edward Larocque Tinker's novel *Toucoutou* (New York: Dodd and Mead, 1928).

Our People and Our History

This case attracted attention because many people in doubt about their origin had been turning to the law to establish a desirable identity. Persons who proved their civil status in court passed as white and enjoyed the rights and privileges accorded this standing. An adverse decision on the other hand proved disastrous, fatal, because it resulted in the loss of all prestige for the complainant, who never again could live under the same social conditions.

These circumstances created division among our people. Some approved, others disapproved the idea of wishing to pass into white society. The dissidents were in the majority, and Beaumont, although a quadroon, was in full sympathy with that group. It was thus he became interested in this famous case for which he acted as historian.

Unfortunately, we do not have all the poems that Beaumont composed relative to this occasion, but we trust the following extracts will suffice to prove his genius and to show how our people reacted to the foolish controversy over the color of the skin. The poet explains the beginning of the trouble thus:

> My master flew like a teal
> Coming out of Bonfuca.
> He came to bring the news;
> To take his sister in his arms;
> To say: "Dear Toucoutou,
> I think we are going crazy."

The sister indignant answered:

> What's all this talk about
> Here in my parlor?
> Why do you speak thus to me?
> Like an evil vagabond?
> A white person! Ah, are you crazy?...
> My name is not Toucoutou.

Then, the philosopher-brother explains to his exasperated sister that some people of color who were trying to pass them-

A Tribute to the Creole People of Color

selves off as white were exposed to the contempt of their neighbors. The poet says this:

> Oh well, dear Anastasia,
> When the Negro tries to be white,
> Society will finish him,
> You better hide under a tin plate.

On another occasion during the prosecution, Anastasia, believing she saw advantages on her side, put on an air of disdain. She threatened her frightened adversary as indicated in the lines:

> She looked at poor Eglantine,
> Who was almost dying of strain,
> And said to her: "My stubborn one,
> You will really know me tomorrow."

Anastasia lost the case. Her brother came to tell her the bad news, saying that he had been present and had heard the judgment of the court from the very mouth of the judges:

> I visited the Court Supreme,
> To see what they were doing,
> I heard the judges and the lawyers say
> That we have lost the suing.

But the most popular song Beaumont composed at the time of the trial of Toucoutou is the one in which he interprets the spirit of the people. In this remarkable composition, Beaumont uses all the irony of his joking nature. After showing how the Negroes would be unhappy if Anastasia had succeeded, he tells of the prestige and social advantages she has lost and ends by hoping that the lesson would serve as an example. Here are the couplets just as they have come down to us:

> TOUCOUTOU
>
> If you win your lawsuit
> Indeed, O Negress, this is bad;
> Bad for those who force it
> And the harm cannot be disregarded.

> Refrain: Ah, Toucoutou, we know you!
> You are a little Mooress.
> Who does not know you?
> No soap will make you white.
>
> At the theater, if you go there,
> Like all white people should,
> They will treat you like Jacdeloge,
> Who did not pass so well as white, did he?
>
> Refrain: Ah, Toucoutou....
>
> When these white lawyers give a dance
> Will you be able to go?
> Will you, O beautiful devil,
> You who love to dance so!
>
> Refrain: Ah, Toucoutou....
>
> I have finished my little song
> Because I want to sleep;
> But I think the lesson will serve,
> For a long time to keep you meek.
>
> Refrain: Ah, Toucoutou....[2]

The lesson did not serve the purpose the poet thought it would. One can say that Beaumont was the Béranger of the Creole people.[3]

Lolo Mansion

We had the honor of knowing Mr. Lolo Mansion.[4] It was indeed a privilege to be in the company of such a man. This venerable

---

2. "Toucoutou" exposed the attempt by a young girl (nicknamed Toucoutou), whose features concealed her Negro ancestry, to pass into the ranks of the whites. She was what the Creoles of color called a *blanc-fo'ce* or *passe-a-blanc*. In order to support her claim of being white, she brought action for libel against a jealous neighbor who had publicly accused her of having Negro blood. The case reached the Louisiana Supreme Court, where Toucoutou lost her appeal. Joseph Beaumont, a barber with a talent for songwriting, voiced in brutal words the contempt and envy that the black population of New Orleans felt toward those of their color who tried to "pass" as white. Edward Larocque Tinker, *Creole City: Its Past and Its People* (New York: Longmans, Green, 1953), 241–42.

3. Pierre Jean Béranger (1780–1857) was a French songwriter and author of light popular verse. During his lifetime, he was regarded as the national poet of France. Paul Harvey and Janet Heseltine (eds.), *The Oxford Companion to French Literature* (Oxford: Clarendon Press, 1959), 85.

4. "Lolo" was Lucien Mansion's nickname. He was the great-grandfather

A Tribute to the Creole People of Color

fellow attracted us not only by his gracious ways but more so by his talent and by his patriotic sentiments.

As we all know, Mansion was the intimate friend of the poet Joanni Questy. They were two sensible, virtuous men whose friendship lasted until death. Both men occupied themselves with the art of writing and with the betterment of humanity. Both were good, wise men. They tell us that in 1855 the persecution launched against the Creoles was particularly hostile. We know that Mr. Mansion generously donated a part of his fortune for the relief of our people and a number of them profited by his generosity, escaping the hardships of prejudice. Mexico and Haiti opened their doors to them and, thanks to the generosity of Mr. Mansion, the unhappy exiles were able to enjoy the advantages of liberty and security in friendly countries.[5] We trust that coming generations will remember the deeds of this good man.

Mansion composed several poems that evidence exquisite taste and quality. His writings offer criticisms of the customs of his day and describe the actual life of his era. It is strange that the merit of such a writer received so little appreciation. He is not even mentioned in *Les Cenelles*. But he had the honor of seeing his name listed in the *Athénée Louisianais* where "La Folle" was published. This unexpected honor brought glory to his name as well as to our people. So long as Louisiana has a literary history and so long as this literary history attracts the attention of people of taste, the renown and glory of Lolo Mansion will live. It is worthwhile noting that his name was saved from oblivion only through the sympathetic consideration of a group completely unknown to the population of color. There were other writers whose works in prose or in verse could have been thus honored through such publicity. Alas, today, these works are lost in oblivion.

---

of Professor Charles Barthélemy Roussève. Mansion's works were published in *L'Union*, in *La Tribune*, and in *Le Crusader*. Charles Barthélemy Roussève, *The Negro in Louisiana: Aspects of His History and His Literature* (New Orleans: Xavier University Press, 1937), 66, 129.

5. The migration of free people of color had begun early in the century. They fled mostly to northern parts of the United States, to France, Mexico, and the West Indies. *Ibid.*, 48.

Our People and Our History

Paul Trévigne

Paul Trévigne was born in New Orleans in 1825. His father was a veteran of 1814–1815. His mother's family name was Découdreau. Trévigne in his youth received a complete, a well-rounded education. He became a teacher and practiced this profession for forty years in the Third District of New Orleans. A linguist, Paul Trévigne spoke and wrote in several languages. He was the close friend of many highly educated men, among whom were Joanni Questy and Basile Crocker [Crokère], one of the most celebrated fencing masters of our city in the past century.[6] Even though Trévigne produced good students, not one of them achieved fame in the literary field. This was undoubtedly because of the changes in attitude prevalent among our people. Several of his students were officers in the Union army, where they distinguished themselves by their intelligence and bravery.

Mr. Trévigne was often called upon to defend the rights of man with his pen. First of all, he was chosen editor in chief of the newspaper *L'Union*, published in New Orleans in the stormy days of 1865. There is no doubt he recognized the grave personal dangers to which he was exposed in this position. He was later invited to serve as editor of *La Tribune*, the daily newspaper founded by Dr. Louis Roudanez.[7] In these new capacities, Trévigne developed his talents to the highest degree.

Mr. Trévigne was involved in a long, perilous battle at *La Tribune*, during which his position called for great courage, talent, and patriotism. As recompense he had only the satisfaction of knowing that his duty was done to the best of his ability. He stayed at his controversial post, serving his people until the newspaper ceased publication [1869]. In the columns of *Louisianian*, a paper of former Governor Pinchback, there appeared under Trévigne's name a literary article entitled "Centennial Tribute."[8] This article commemorated the one-hundredth an-

---

6. Basile Crokère is discussed in Chapter VI, below.
7. See Chapter XI, note 9, below.
8. Pinckney Benton Stewart Pinchback, the black lieutenant governor of Louisiana, filled the vacancy left at the death of black Governor Oscar J. Dunn. He was acting governor from December, 1872, to January, 1873, dur-

A Tribute to the Creole People of Color

niversary of American independence, celebrated in 1866 with an exposition [Centennial Exposition] in Philadelphia. It discussed the works of old Creoles and was written in English.

From 1892 to 1896, *Le Crusader* enjoyed Trévigne as a collaborator.[9] He edited the French section of this paper and translated current articles published daily in its columns.

Trévigne had a concise yet easy-going style. He laughed as he chastised with his satire. Perhaps this playful manner with which he communicated his ideas and his thinking served to spare him disagreeable reprisals, particularly at a time when white people were little accustomed to accepting the opinions of a man of color. Nothing fired the indignation of the Democrat so much as the sight of a man of color holding a position of prominence in the intellectual world. All that he could say, do, or write to defend his cause, to emphasize his progress, or to prove his ability, was only another sign of his impertinence; and the hatred for a man like Trévigne was ever intense and ready to burst into flame at the least provocation. Mr. Trévigne died at the age of eighty-three.

His long life afforded him the opportunity of witnessing the great crises of our country. Trévigne was born and grew up during the period of slavery. Highly educated and endowed with a keen intellect, he was capable of following and evaluating the events that unfolded before him. He saw his people—men, women, and children—sold on the slave block. He saw them flogged, he saw them suffer and die in chains. Later he saw the light of liberty break through, and this motivated him deeply

---

ing Governor Henry Clay Warmoth's impeachment. E. Merton Coulter, *The South During Reconstruction, 1865–1877* (Baton Rouge: Louisiana State University Press, 1947), 143, 352.

9. *Le Crusader*, edited by Trévigne, was the successor to *La Tribune* and was the official voice of the Citizens' Committee in waging legal battles against post-Reconstruction discrimination. It was founded in 1890 by Louis A. Martinet, a committee member. The paper appeared first as a weekly, then as a daily; it was discontinued in 1897. Rodolphe Desdunes, Paul Trévigne, and Numa E. Mansion (son of Lucien Mansion) contributed regularly to its columns in French and in English. Edward Larocque Tinker, *Les écrits de langue française en Louisiane au XIXe siècle* (Paris: Libraire Ancienne Honoré Champion, 1932), 475.

with a compulsion to share the experiences of his long life. This he did, and our people therefore owe him a place among the immortals. Trévigne always cherished the respect and the trust we placed in him.

The grave must not efface the memory of Trévigne's merit, hence we have chosen to memorialize him. There may be other men who surpass Paul Trévigne, but his life, a eulogy in itself, speaks for him. Trévigne's position was one never before accorded any of his compatriots. The truth of history is the nourishing mother of justice.

Adolphe Duhart

Following these men of 1844, there was in New Orleans another type of distinguished Creole of color, several in number. Circumstances then were such that these men had to follow diverse paths. A leader among these was Adolphe Duhart. He was a poet and an author whose drama *Lelia* was staged at the Orleans Theater about 1867.[10] He was educated in France and succeeded Joanni Questy as principal of the school for Negro orphans.[11] He died about two years ago [ca. 1908]. His beautiful poetry won for him the soubriquet, "Favorite of the Gods." Armand Duhart, his brother, was a skilled printer and also a man of literary talent.

Armand died in 1905, leaving behind him the name of a man of honor and of wealth. He was one of the directors of the Bernard Couvent institute and a member of the Louisiana Union, founded in 1884, whose purpose was to assist the Couvent institute and to contribute generally to the intellectual and moral growth of the people.

---

10. A native New Orleanian, Duhart also wrote for *La Tribune* under the name "Lelia." *Ibid.*
11. See notes 3 and 4, Chapter IV.

Chapter VI
The Creole of Color in the Arts and the Liberal Arts Professions ∽ A Page in Our Political History ∽ Popular Military Men ∽ Figures of the Past

Eugène Warbourg

Eugène Warbourg was born in New Orleans about 1825 and died in Rome in 1861. He grew up in his native city, where he was able to develop his talents as a sculptor. Warbourg received his first lessons from a French artist by the name of Gabriel, whose studio was located on Bourbon Street. Gabriel must have been a very generous person, because he braved prejudice in order to develop the young Creole's talents. Under the direction of this able and conscientious man, Warbourg made rapid and remarkable progress. His work soon attracted attention.

Later, when he undertook to work for his livelihood, he encountered no difficulty whatsoever in winning an appreciative clientele. People of influence encouraged him. They entrusted to him the execution of exceedingly delicate works. He received commissions for busts of generals, magistrates, and other notables. The old cemeteries of New Orleans are filled with masterpieces from Warbourg's hands. Among his more famous pieces of sculpture is a statue of two angels carved from a solid block of marble. Each angel holds in its right hand a chalice; the whole rests on a common base. The creation of this statue was judged so delicate an undertaking that others refrained from attempting to produce it. Warbourg's reputation was established through the fulfilling of this commission. When the person who had ordered the statue did not claim it, the artist felt he should dispose of it. It is said that a man by the name of Panniston bought the masterpiece.

Warbourg also accepted contracts from the clergy, for whom he executed magnificent works of art. The St. Louis Cathedral, the Hotels Grunewald and Herman housed some of his exquisite creations. His success aroused jealousy among his competitors, who became his arch enemies. Warbourg's studio on St. Peter Street between Bourbon and Royal was next to that of his brother Daniel, who also was an artist of merit and Warbourg's assistant. For some time the two brothers ignored the hostility directed toward them, but in the end they lost hope that the situation would ever improve. Eugène bade New Orleans good-bye; he sailed for Europe in 1852.

First, he went to Paris where he studied sculpture for six years. Next, he traveled to Belgium, but his stay there was of short duration. He then went to England. In London he met the Duchess of S____, who engaged him to make some bas-reliefs representing scenes from Harriet Beecher Stowe's *Uncle Tom's Cabin*. He worked for a year on this project, and on its completion left London for Florence with the full intention of settling there. But when he discovered in this center of art the same disagreeable conditions as those he had suffered in his own country, he set out for Rome. In the Eternal City, Warbourg found the happiness he was seeking, but only for a short time. There, in Italy's capital city, at the early age of thirty-six, Warbourg died, only two years after his arrival.

Warbourg's genius endowed the world of art with several productions that made him more than famous. Newspapers on two continents carried stories of his works. Artists and savants acclaimed his creativity with sympathy and respectful admiration. Warbourg and [Norbert] Rillieux were without question the two best-known Louisianians in Europe. *The Fisherman* and *The First Kiss* are named as Warbourg's most outstanding works.

Daniel Warbourg

Daniel Warbourg, Eugène's brother, lived to do honor to the name he bore because of his achievements in marble carving. He likewise was an engraver. Daniel, Jr., is another member of this family so favored by nature. He is considered as an accomplished artist in granite and marble sculpture. If he were not a man of color, he would long ago have occupied the place due him because of his talents. He has produced some works of admirable elegance and incontestable merit.

[Daniel] Warbourg was a free man of color, a child of foreign-born parents. His status of birth permitted him to educate himself and to develop his talents, a privilege not accorded to slaves. Let us note here in passing that certain writers never fail to talk at length about the talents of Negroes as dancers, but the reader will search in vain among the works of these same authors to find a single line about the genius of such men as the Warbourgs.

Alexandre Pickhil

We had our Titian in Louisiana in the person of Alexandre Pickhil. We know that Pickhil produced magnificent pictures, but he has left us nothing as a legacy, perhaps because he became disillusioned. He is said to have executed a full-length portrait of an eminent ecclesiastic, but he destroyeyd this masterpiece because of vicious criticism passed upon it. Thus, although Pickhil may have been the best painter of his era, he preferred to die in misery and anonymity rather than display his talent to the detriment of his self-respect. He died in New Orleans about the middle of the past century, between 1840 and 1850. It is said that disillusionment cast a cloud of despair over his whole life.

Joseph Abeilard

Joseph Abeilard was one of the most skillful architects Louisiana produced before the War of Secession. He was an accomplished artisan. He could create a plan as though he were an educated architect, select the correct materials as though he were a stonecutter, and draw up an agreement as though he truly were a contractor. Next, he could execute these plans with the professional skill of a master builder. Abeilard was known to have worked in all these different capacities.

His talent in architecture won recognition for him but, sad to say, the prestige rightfully due him was quickly snatched from his grasp. He accepted work under men who were totally incapable but who enjoyed the advantage of being white. The *Marché Bazar* and the Sugar Sheds located on our city's riverfront were examples of the work in question. Abeilard's genius provided the talent for the successful completion of these buildings, but the contract for them was given to another man for his sole profit. This false architect had the good sense to employ Abeilard, who saw that everything was properly done, permitting the other man to collect his fees without effort.

Many of our older citizens remember Abeilard. We feel sure that their judgment of his merits is the same as ours. His talent in architecture definitely contributed to the beautification of our city. For more than forty years he worked as a designer and builder.

He was born in New Orleans and died there. His brother Jules was also an artisan of distinction. Although not the equal of Joseph, he too possessed a wealth of ability that he brought to important assignments in the city, assignments entrusted exclusively to him because of his extraordinary gift. Jules died in Panama, leaving behind an enviable reputation.

E. J. Edmunds

We must eulogize the name of Professor E. J. Edmunds. Born in New Orleans, he died at a rather young age. He was a skilled mathematician. On his return from school in France, state authorities quickly profited from his talents. About the year 1872, the Public School Office invited him to occupy the chair of mathematics at the New Orleans High School and he accepted at once.

As always, the newspapers attacked him. This was a calculated ruse to make sure the newly chosen instructor was capable of carrying out the exacting functions that he had assumed. The battle between the press and the young professor was of short duration. In order to end the annoyance, the master challenged all of his detractors to meet him at the blackboard. After that, they left him alone.

A Tribute to the Creole People of Color

Professor Edmunds lost his mind as a result of a grievous illness. Like Mr. Nelson Fouché, he was a scholar in mathematics and he was also an expert in astronomy. We regret that such a capable man died so young.

Norbert Rillieux

Norbert Rillieux [1806–94] was the most famous of the Creoles. We have produced heroes, writers, musicians, painters, sculptors, and architects, but Rillieux was a scientific genius. The invention of his vacuum pan was one of the most revolutionizing advances in the sugar refining industry.[1] It introduced into the manufacture of sugar a procedure that not only made for a better product, but greatly assisted the planters in their operations. Efforts were made to duplicate his invention, but to no avail.

A Mr. Stackhouse, owner of a factory, employed a man who posed as an engineer and pretended he could supply a substitute for Rillieux's vacuum pan. Mr. Stackhouse, falsely led by bold assurances, gave the imposter permission to proceed with the building of a better device. His mistake cost him dearly. The bogus "inventor" demolished piece by piece the entire apparatus of Rillieux's machine, only to discover he could not replace it or even rebuild it. In despair Stackhouse was compelled to secure the services of a skilled workman who, with the aid of Mr. Orville Marigny, a skilled mechanic, finally succeeded in reassembling the parts of Rillieux's machine.

In the applied sciences, Norbert Rillieux had no equal in Louisiana. Possessing innate knowledge as well as acquired training in construction, he was a genius at invention and adept

---

1. The refining process then in use was slow and costly. In 1846 Rillieux developed evaporating machinery that improved the method extensively. Because his invention was not readily accepted by Louisiana's sugar producers, he returned to France in 1854. Europeans also responded negatively at first to the new method. After about ten years, Europeans with sugar plantations in the West Indies began to experiment with his process and subsequently adopted it, opening the way for the revolution in the sugar industry. Wilhelmena S. Robinson, *Historical Negro Biographies* (New York: Publishers Co., Inc., 1969), 117–18.

in executing his plans. It was said that his advice was as valuable as was the stroke of his hammer. But despite Rillieux's genius, despite the benefits that his services rendered to Louisiana's principal industry, he was made to feel the sting of humiliation and prejudice because of his race.

After his death the papers of New Orleans pretended to sing his praises, but they never once referred to him as a black man and all intelligent persons understood the reason for this despicable silence. It was considered important to deprive the Creoles of the glory they could have enjoyed from the illustrious contributions he rendered to society.

But as the head of the Central School in Paris, Norbert Rillieux was indeed appreciated. There he held the rank proper for a man of his value. No matter what attitude persisted in his own country, regardless of the silence of vicious, ungrateful people, Rillieux's place in history will never be forgotten.

It is said that he had submitted to the city certain specifications for the building of canals, but the question of race caused these plans to be rejected by the city authorities.[2] We have no reason to doubt this report, for prejudice has caused many stupidities in our country. The judgment of even enlightened people can be warped, as was demonstrated by the Stackhouse incident.

Antoine Dubuclet

The injustice of prejudice was never more manifest than in the attitude of the Louisiana people toward the Honorable Antoine Dubuclet, treasurer of the state from 1868 to 1879. During this whole stormy period, Mr. Dubuclet directed the finances of Louisiana. After eleven years of service, he retired without leaving behind the least cause for dissatisfaction or any error in his accounts. What we state here has been confirmed through extremely hostile and scrutinizing inquiry. Some of the most

---

2. Rillieux designed a method for handling sewage that, incidentally, would have removed much of the menace of yellow fever from New Orleans, but his plans were not adopted. *Ibid.*

A Tribute to the Creole People of Color

eminent politicians of Louisiana came—determined to find irregularities in Dubuclet's records, but to no avail. The Aldiger Committee was at this time actually created for the one purpose of examining Dubuclet's accounts.[3]

The men of the committee, in order to achieve their end, secured the services of three of the most reliable experts in the field of accounting. For six months the investigation continued. The group made every effort to prove Dubuclet guilty but his integrity prevailed. In any other case, a person who had proved himself so clean would have been given high commendation but not Dubuclet, for he was a Creole of color.

Despite the embezzlement and ignominies that marked the administration of state finances during this period, no one had enough loyalty to this model official to offer the slightest praise for his fine civic qualities.

"O Athenians, how much it costs to be praised by you!"

Oscar Guimbillotte

Dr. Guimbillotte was the son of a Frenchman and a woman of color. He had every appearance of being a white man and numbered many friends among the people of that race. He married a person of color and lived without ever being embarrassed over his origin. He practiced his profession dutifully for more than twenty-five years and lavished his services upon everyone without discrimination.

Guimbillotte honored the Creole population by his extensive charity, his versatility, and his thorough knowledge of medicine. He was a conscientious physician. He was not content with paying professional visits to his patients and presenting

---

3. When Governor William Pitt Kellogg was removed from office, State Treasurer Dubuclet, a black man, was the only one of his cabinet allowed to remain in office. Kellogg had opposed Dubuclet because of his race. Stuart Omer Landry, *The Battle of Liberty Place: The Overthrow of Carpet-Bag Rule in New Orleans, September 14, 1874* (New Orleans: Pelican Publishing Co., 1955), 49–50. Dubuclet was investigated in 1875 by the committee of inquiry (Aldiger), with United States Chief Justice Edward Douglass White as chairman. White reported no errors in the accounts. James T. Rapier, "Rebuilding Waste Places after the War," *Negro History Bulletin*, I, No. 7 (April, 1938).

his bill, but he also brought to their homes his sympathy and his understanding. Often he prepared the medications and administered them himself, and watched over the patient at his bedside in order to verify the effects of his treatment. This procedure saved the life of many a patient whose condition needed the attention and surveillance of an eye schooled in medical science.

Dr. Guimbillotte proved his merit and won the hearts of many respectable families who held for him eternal gratitude. They say that he was interested in medicinal herbs and that he never hesitated to make use of these on certain occasions when the usual medicines did not produce the desired results. The doctor was also a man of letters: he had studied in Paris. People who knew him said that he possessed a prodigious memory, that his knowledge of literature was as stupendous as was his scientific acumen.

Dr. Guimbillotte's death was a heavy loss to us. He had a kindly face, and, as stated, he possessed European or Caucasian features. He had large blue eyes and a high forehead. His long, silky brown hair fell in thick locks over his broad shoulders. Although not of large stature, he was of athletic build. His strength and noble mien attracted everyone. He died January 21, 1886, at the age of fifty-five.

Alexandre Chaumette

Dr. Alexandre Chaumette, although a native of New Orleans, spent his youth in Paris, where he received his medical education. He has the distinction of being the first colored doctor to come to New Orleans as a practicing physician. In fact, his arrival in our city created quite a stir. The other doctors, whether because of prejudice or dislike, perhaps for both reasons, opposed his practice. They initiated a humiliating examination for him, but because Chaumette was fortified with a recognized diploma from France, he could not be forced to submit to this ordeal. He therefore was finally admitted to the practice of

A Tribute to the Creole People of Color

medicine in our city. Our people benefited from his skill as a doctor and from the contributions he offered as a citizen.

Doctor Chaumette conducted some serious studies. If his work was finally recognized by the medical fraternity of this city, it was because of the ample proof that he had given of his great knowledge. He had been attached to hospital service in Paris, where, as an intern, he had acquired vast experience.

The persecution finally ceased, and Dr. Chaumette won the confidence both of the whites and the blacks.[4]

Basile Crokère

Basile Crokère was a remarkable member of the Creole population. He was born in New Orleans and it was there that he developed his talents, particularly as a fencing master. He was likewise a skilled mathematician and a craftsman of some reputation.

Mr. Crokère, like a number of his compatriots, applied himself both to work and to study. In time, thanks to his intelligence and courage, he was able to overcome the difficulties of his environment.

As a carpenter he became one of the most skilled builders of staircases in New Orleans. Only one other man was his equal in this trade, his friend Noël J. Bacchus. It was, however, because of his success as a swordsman and as a mathematician that he won the honor he holds today in the history of distinguished men of Louisiana.[5]

---

4. Chaumette ranks with other early prominent black physicians in the United States, among whom was Dr. James Derham of Philadelphia, the first Negro doctor to practice in this country. Derham had been the slave of a physician, a Dr. Robert of New Orleans, who helped him gain his freedom. Derham (latter part of eighteenth century) was followed by Chaumette, Louis Charles Roudanez and his two sons, Louis and Charles. Dr. James T. Newman, born in Louisiana in 1846, was a member of the staff of visiting surgeons at Charity Hospital from 1872 until 1877. All of these men had large practices among both races. Charles Barthélemy Rousséve, *The Negro in New Orleans* (New Orleans: Archives of Negro History, Inc., 1969), 9–10.

5. His *Salle d'Armes* was always crowded with students. The Creole gentry did not scruple to cross swords with him in private assaults even though prejudice versus men of color existed. Crokère was one of the handsomest

Our People and Our History

As a fencing master, Crokère attracted the attention of the general public. Although the population counted among them a number of experts in this art, Basile Crokère was proclaimed superior to all. It has been said that he won this reputation in the fencing schools and not on the dueling ground. This is perhaps because he spent hours teaching youths the use and knowledge of weapons.

Crokère was an educated and respectable man who won esteem because of his good character, his conduct, and his polished manners. It is not strange that a man possessing these commendable qualities should enjoy a certain regard among the upper classes of society, among whom he created an elite clientele.

The Creole population is proud to have produced a man like Basile Crokère, a man who, without leaving the place of his birth, acquired enough renown to receive the praise of all ranks of society.

He was known also as a most successful mathematics teacher. As for his prowess in the use of weapons, it is said he could touch his adversary even while composing a ballad, as did [Edmond] Rostand's hero [Cyrano de Bergerac]. He often said that his chest was a sacred spot. It seemed this was actually true, for it was never even pinked by his opponent's blade.

---

men of New Orleans. With dignity he walked down the street in his green broadcloth suit with spotless linen and the widest of black stocks around his neck. He was famous for his collection of cameos. He wore cameo rings, breast pin, and even a cameo bracelet. Annie Lee West-Stahl, "The Free Negro in Ante-Bellum Louisiana," *Louisiana Historical Quarterly*, XXV (April, 1942), 373. Crokère's home was at the corner of Exchange Alley and Constitution Street, just opposite the courthouse. "Visitors to City Find Great Store of Historic Sights," *Times-Picayune*, (XCVI, No. 11, 2-4, 1932).

Crokère is listed in all city directories as a free man of color. His white father sent him to Paris for his education; there he fought numerous duels before returning to the United States. Harnett T. Kane, *Queen New Orleans: City by the River* (New York: William Morrow, 1949), 158.

Little has been preserved on Crokère, whose name was often spelled differently: Bazile, Basil, Bazil, Basile, Crokère, Crocker, Croker, Croquer, Croquière.

Crokère was seventy-nine at his death; he was survived by his wife. *L'Abeille de la Nouvelle-Orléans*, obituary, January 30, 1879.

A Tribute to the Creole People of Color

Moreover, Crokère understood, as did his most respected compatriots, that labor, even manual labor, has value.

It seems apropos to state that during Crokère's time there lived other noted duelists. The best known are Robert Séverin, St. Pierre, Joseph Joly, and Joseph Auld. These swordsmen were the companions and followers of the great master, and on more than one occasion they crossed swords with him. Dueling was in style at this time but this noble pastime, like all the others, had to give way to the new order of things introduced into our social life by the events of the War of Secession of 1861.[6]

Mr. Crokère possessed personal charm. His conversation was always engaging and articulate, and because of this his company was sought after. Needless to say he contributed significantly to the prestige of the Creole population. Among his intimate friends, he numbered Professors Trévigne and Questy, distinguished compatriots of the highest intellectual caliber. One was the editor of *La Tribune*,[7] the other was a disciple of Apollo.

In one history book on Louisiana, Mr. Basile Crokère is listed as a mulatto. This is an error. He was a quadroon. The term "mulatto" is so offensive to us that we prefer to be more precise. In a certain context, the word even carries infamous connotations.

François Boisdoré

François Boisdoré, a talented orator, engaged in frequent debates for the Republican cause. At the beginning of Reconstruction, in 1868, he acquired distinction because of his eloquent speeches in our political assemblies. We must say that Mr. Boisdoré brought honor to the Creole population because of his patriotism, his high character, and the active part he took in

---

6. Fencing was a popular pre-Civil War pastime; dueling was the gentleman's way of settling disputes. A number of black New Orleanians achieved skill in this art, and the proudest whites did not hesitate to be taught by black masters of the sword who taught only white pupils. John Smith Kendall, "According to the Code," *Louisiana Historical Quarterly*, XXIII (January, 1940), 146.

7. See Chapter XI, below.

public debates when the cause of progress had need of capable and zealous defenders. We owe this eulogy to his memory.

For a long time, he was bookkeeper for Mr. Pierre Cazenave, the leading undertaker and embalmer in New Orleans during the mid-1880's. It is said Mr. Cazenave carried to his grave a secret formula for preserving a corpse indefinitely. We believe this to be true, for there exists today at Emile Labat's establishment a mummy embalmed by Cazenave that has never shown the least signs of deterioration.

Cazenave's funeral home, where Mr. Boisdoré worked for so many years, was located at the corner of Bourbon and St. Louis streets. It seems hardly necessary to add that Mr. Boisdoré belonged to the free population of antebellum times and that he possessed an excellent education. At Pierre Cazenave's death, Boisdoré was forced to change his profession. This is why he became a school teacher shortly after the Civil War.

Mr. Boisdoré was a handsome man, striking in appearance. He was circumspect, serious, and careful in his speech, seldom indulging in pleasantries or jokes of any sort. With Boisdoré's death, the Creole people lost a highly educated confrere, one who was strong, honest, and useful. He died about ten years ago.

FIGURES OF THE PAST

François Escoffié, Séverin Lataure, and Léoni Monthieu were professors of renown, highly esteemed for the services they rendered to our people as school men. Soulié, Delassize, Boré, the Rillieuxs, brothers of the inventor, the Hewletts, St. Amants, Sincyrs, Barjons, Fonvergenes, Beauvers, Brulés, Castelins, and many others likewise were persons of position and quality.

Some signalized themselves in business, others in industry, but all possessed enviable reputations. It is proper to list these men because they have brought honor and prestige to the Creoles of color. Each is justifiably recognized for his merits. Unfortunately, the prejudice of some people and the heedless-

A Tribute to the Creole People of Color

ness of others seem to have erected a barrier of silence around their illustrious names. But this silence will not always endure. The future will probably inquire into the past. It is to be supposed that the men of tomorrow will ask about the men of yesterday. In this case may this modest work serve as an aid to those who wish to know more about them.

Joseph Colastin Rousseau

Mr. Joseph Colastin Rousseau was a native of New Orleans, a man of the past century who devoted much of his time to the study of literature. We have a pamphlet of his, entitled *Les Contemporains* [*The Contemporaries*], wherein he portrays graciously and attractively his experience with the people of his time. He wrote only prose. Even though he is not one of the collaborators in *Les Cenelles,* he is equal to any of those intellectual men who contributed to this famous book.[8]

He left for Haiti a little before the war of 1861 and later adopted that country as his homeland. There he studied law and became an attorney. His success before the bar of the Black Republic was certainly remarkable, for people still talk about it.

He left no heirs. His wife was Miss Populus, a granddaughter of the celebrated [Major Joseph] Savary who commanded the Haitians in the battle on the plains of Chalmette against the English during the war of 1814–15.[9]

---

8. Rousseau, son of one of the wealthiest and most distinguished black families, wrote both prose and verse. Rousseve, citing Edward Larocque Tinker, *Les écrits de langue française en Louisiane au XIXᵉ siècle* (Paris: Libraire Ancienne Honoré Champion, 1932), 424.

9. Joseph Savary was a Haitian from Santo Domingo. He organized the Second Battalion of Free Men of Color which fought under General Jackson (but was led by a white officer, Major Louis Daquin, according to Jackson's policy) in 1814–15. For his distinguished service, Savary was appointed by Jackson to the rank of second major, the first black in the ranks to be thus honored. Roland C. McConnell, *Negro Troops of Antebellum Louisiana: A History of the Battalion of Free Men of Color* (Baton Rouge: Louisiana State University Press, 1968), 69–71, 109.

On October 12, 1812, Governor Claiborne of Louisiana, upon reactivating the black militia, had appointed Isidore Honoré, a free man of color, second lieutenant in this group, the first example of a state's commissioning a black officer. *Ibid.*, 53.

Chapter VII
Music and the Creoles of Color ⁂ Rivalry Among Artists ⁂ Prejudice

MUSIC AMONG THE CREOLES OF COLOR

The Creoles of color have produced excellent musicians and composers. But the Lambert family, the father and his two sons, surpassed all the others, both in Louisiana and abroad.[1] The father was proclaimed the most famous of the three. Unfortunately, he has left us nothing, possibly because during his lifetime, Louisiana was too primitive to appreciate this musical genius. His sons won applause in Paris, Portugal, and Brazil. Lucien was particularly outstanding. He produced a number of compositions, which he dedicated to distinguished people in those countries. The nobility did not disdain these dedications.

For a long time, the Lamberts enjoyed popularity in Louisiana, but like so many others, they left the United States for places that offered richer opportunities. As distinguished pianists they performed in the Orleans Theater, where other noted artists were pleased to participate in their concerts. Among these was the renowned Gottschalk.[2] Despite all the changes

---

1. Lambert was a prominent name in New Orleans music from 1840 to 1879 and even afterward. One Richard Lambert taught music in Louisiana. A. E. Perkins (ed.), *Who's Who in Colored Louisiana* (Baton Rouge: Douglas Loan Co., Inc., 1930), 75. His sons Lucien and Sidney, both excellent pianists, became court musicians in Brazil and Portugal, respectively. Maud Cuney-Hare, *Negro Musicians and Their Music* (Washington, D.C.: The Associated Press, 1936), 236. John Lambert, born in 1862, was a well-known cornetist in New Orleans; and an E. Lambert and two Misses Lambert were prominent piano teachers. James M. Trotter, *Music and Some Highly Musical People* (Boston: Lee and Shepard, 1878), 338–40.

The "Philharmonic Society," which was active about 1876, was composed of a group of trained musicians under the direction of experienced teachers and conductors such as Richard Lambert and Constantin Deburque. This all-black group of instrumentalists was organized for the presentation of classical music.

2. Louis Moreau Gottschalk, American composer and pianist, was born

A Tribute to the Creole People of Color

that have intervened since the Civil War, there are still those who have not forgotten what took place at these artistic gatherings. There are few survivors left from those interesting years, but the voice of tradition brings us echoes of that time. Among other things we have heard that there existed a small artistic rivalry between Gottschalk and Lambert, and that this rivalry was controlled by the intervention of mutual friends who commended each genius equally and gave the same credit to each.

Gottschalk was recognized as superior to Lambert as an instrumentalist; Lambert surpassed Gottschalk as a composer. In those days there was no question about the respective merits of each in his own field.

Eugène Macarty

Mr. Eugène Macarty was an excellent pianist.[3] More fortunate than his contemporaries, he won quick public recognition both because of his personality and because of his popular composi-

---

in New Orleans, May 8, 1829; he died in Rio de Janeiro, December 18, 1869. His father was an English broker; his mother was the daughter of refugees from Santo Domingo. Gottschalk was educated in Paris. He wrote many compositions, including a symphony, an overture, a cantata, and two unproduced operas. He is remembered today for his sentimental piano pieces, such as "The Last Hope," "The Dying Poet," "Bamboula," and "The Banjo," which show the Creole tradition. Vernon Loggins, *Where the Word Ends: The Life of Louis Moreau Gottschalk* (Baton Rouge: Louisiana State University Press, 1958), 3–8, 47–79, and *passim*.

Felix Kuntz states that Gottschalk was the first American concert artist to win acclaim in Europe. He claims that the musician came back to New Orleans only once, in 1853, when he gave a concert, assisted by musicians from the French Opera troupe, who were appearing at the Orleans Theater. Kuntz, *250 Years of Life in New Orleans* (New Orleans: Friends of the Cabildo, Louisiana State Museum, 1968), 54.

3. Macarty was born in New Orleans in 1821 and studied piano under J. Norres. In 1840 the French ambassador to the United States recommended him as a pupil in voice, harmony, and composition at the Conservatory of Paris. Macarty was also a writer of prose and verse and a businessman of substantial means. Maud Cuney-Hare, "Musical Pioneers," in Lindsay Patterson (ed.), *The Negro in Music and Art* (New York: Publishers Co., Inc., 1967), 175. Macarty performed at the Orleans Theater during a program, "Vaudeville," honoring Samuel Snaër in 1865. Donald Everett, "Free Persons of Color in New Orleans, 1803–1865" (Ph.D. dissertation, Tulane University, 1952), 221–23. Macarty published his literary works in *L'Union* and *La Tribune*. Edward Larocque Tinker, *Les écrits de langue française en Louisiane au XIXe siècle* (Paris: Libraire Ancienne Honoré Champion, 1932), 294.

tions. Many claimed he was the only real artist among the Creoles. But according to the critical reports of persons highly respected for their judgment in music circles, Eugène Macarty was not nearly the equal of the Lamberts in the theory of music or in its creation and rendition. However, Macarty's versatility was fantastic. His wide variety of talents included a rich, resonant baritone voice, exquisitely cultivated. He was also a natural comedian, rivaling Charles Vêque, who at that time was considered a comedian of the first order. Vêque had long since risen from the amateur ranks to become a professional actor.

In every stage performance offered by the Creole population, Macarty carried the leading role, which was bestowed on him by common consent. He was the logical successor of Orso, of Villasseau, and of those other artist-performers whose triumphs have left lasting memories in the minds of their contemporaries.

Macarty was also an orator. Blessed with a strong voice and clear diction, his speech was fluent and eloquent. In the first days of the Reconstruction, he often appeared before gatherings of our people to discuss with force and intelligence the questions of our rights and freedom, and he never failed to receive warm applause. One may say, then, that Macarty was a musician, a singer, a speaker, a comedian, and a politician.

Samuel Snaër

Samuel Snaër was perhaps a greater musical savant than was Macarty, but his modesty seriously hampered his talent. In his profession he never became prominent. Although he preferred the violin, he was capable of playing a dozen instruments. Snaër had a beautiful tenor voice but he refused to sing. He was a master in harmony, but his compositions stayed in the bottom of his trunk, where time and insects destroyed them. Before the public Samuel Snaër gave evidence of being a very ordinary instrumentalist; however, to those who knew him intimately he was definitely a musical genius.

He was a native Orleanian, born in 1835, and grew up in our city. He played the organ very well and for years he was organist

A Tribute to the Creole People of Color

at St. Mary's Church on Chartres Street. Too timid to seek publicity and too indolent to break loose through emigration from the shackles that bound him from birth, he fell into a state of apathy and was forgotten long before his death. Today the people speak of Snaër as a chess player and not as the artist he really was.[4]

Edmond Dédé

Edmond Dédé was a black man born in New Orleans about 1829, a contemporary of Macarty and of Snaër. A violin prodigy, he first studied in New Orleans under the tutorship of skillful and conscientious teachers. After having mastered everything in his field available to a black man in the city, he went to Europe on the advice of understanding friends. He visited Belgium first, but not finding in that little kingdom the object of his search, he traveled to Paris, where he received a ready welcome. In this enlightened capital, in which everyone acknowledges talent wherever it exists, Edmond Dédé met with sympathy and assistance. In this hospitable country, he found the opportunity he was seeking, namely, that of perfecting his gift in music and of going as far as he possibly could in his profession as a violinist. Through the intervention of friends, he was soon admitted as an auditioner for the Paris Conservatory of Music. His progress and his triumphs quickly attracted the attention of the musical world, and he was given all the consideration awarded to true merit. He was the conductor of the Theater of Bordeaux for twenty-five years. The violin always remained his instrument.

In 1893 Dédé returned to New Orleans, where he presented a number of concerts. The music critic of *L'Abeille*, among others, honored him by attending one of his performances. He

---

4. Snaër was a master of the violin, cello, organ, piano, and other instruments. Because he preferred to live a secluded life, the public never actually became acquainted with his musical gift. His compositions included "Sous sa Fenêtre [Under Her Window]," "Rapelle-Toi [Remember]," "Le Vampire [The Vampire]," "Le Bohemien [The Bohemian]," and "Le Chant des Canotiers [The Song of the Boatmen]." Cuney-Hare, "Musical Pioneers," 175.

was greatly impressed at seeing Dédé play "Le Trouvère" without a score, and gave him ample praise in the columns of his newspaper.

The ship on which Dédé had booked passage from France to New Orleans had such a rough crossing that the vessel was compelled to seek port on the Texas coast. During this experience Dédé lost his favorite violin, a Cremona. This misfortune, however, did not prevent his appearance in New Orleans—often in concert halls with poor acoustics—where he captivated his audiences even with a borrowed instrument greatly inferior to his lost Cremona. It is said he memorized the works of all the great masters. He has left us two ballads: "Patriotisme" and "Si J'etais Lui [If I Were He]." [5] He should not be judged solely by these compositions. He wrote thousands of such pieces, not counting the dances and the ballets distributed over all parts of Europe where he visited or lived. In Algeria he composed the "Serment de l'Arabe [The Pledge of the Arab]." His compositions were all of high quality. He even began the composition of a grand opera called *Le Sultan d'Ispahan* [The Sultan of Spain], which he never completed because of illness. Edmond Dédé died in Paris in 1903.

Basile Barrès

Here was a Creole of color who was certainly very popular in New Orleans. He was a Frenchman in heart and in spirit—a

---

5. *L'Artiste*, a Bordeaux periodical, states that Dédé was born on November 20, 1827 or 1829, of free parents who had emigrated from the West Indies. In New Orleans he studied under a Negro violinist, C. Deburque and under L. Gabici. He went to Mexico in 1848 for further study; and, with the financial help of friends, entered the Paris Conservatory in 1857, where he was a pupil of Halery and Alard. He mastered the violin. A composer of many orchestral works, he was probably best known for the "Palmier Overture." Other compositions by Dédé are "The Valiant Lovely Rose," "Quadrille," and "Sensitive." He was conductor of the orchestra of L'Acazar in Bordeaux and was an intimate friend of Gounod. After forty-six years in Europe he visited New Orleans, where he was received with honors, but soon returned to France and died in Bordeaux. Charles Barthélemy Roussève, *The Negro in Louisiana: Aspects of His History and His Literature* (New Orleans: Xavier University Press, 1937), 52, 152, 156; Cuney-Hare, *Negro Musicians*, 236–38.

A Tribute to the Creole People of Color

perfect gentleman whom everyone was happy to know.[6] He was a native of our city. When still very young, he entered the employment of Mr. Perrier, the great merchant of French music on Royal Street. There he learned to play the piano and before long became an artist of the first order. Mr. Perrier sent him on several trips to Paris in the interest of his establishment, and Barrès would always return with a greater love than ever for France.

Barrès was a piano-tuner, a music teacher, and a composer. His dance pieces were quite popular in New Orleans. When the great violinist Dédé visited us, it was Basile he chose to accompany him at the piano. Everyone loved Basile: everyone grieved at his death. He left a son and three daughters, who are living here today.

THE EXPERIENCE OF A MUSICIAN

Not long ago there lived in New Orleans an excellent musical composer. Unfortunately, the color of his skin overshadowed his genius each time he was near triumph. People used his talent and took advantage of his kindness and his zeal, but when it was time to recognize his services or honor his talents, those who had been his judges and who had proof of his valor and of his good will remained silent. This conspiracy of silence was unforgiveable. People who employed him, who extended him an invitation, who requested his performances were so filled with prejudice toward his race, that they said not a word of praise or even gave the slightest mark or sign of appreciation, not even a little publicity. Not all were remiss, however, for our musician often received heavy applause from his spectators. Those we accuse here know well the ones who sought him out

---

6. Basile Barrès (also spelled Barès) was born in New Orleans in 1846. He studied music in Paris under Eugène Prevost, director of the *Theatre Orleans*. He gave a piano recital in 1867 while visiting the Paris Exposition. His salon pieces demonstrate effective use of the glissando and embellishment that were in vogue in the period and were found in the Mexican and Spanish-Creole music. Cuney-Hare, "Musical Pioneers," 175.

for orchestration for vaudeville, for operas, and other delicate pieces that no other person would dare try to execute.

They will recall that this young man of superior talent and generous heart not only sought perfection in the arrangement of certain musical scores submitted to him, but also at times he even added to the principal work the graceful beauties of his own creation. They cannot forget the performances the young master executed by invitation, and they salved their consciences by thanking him in secret for the services he had rendered.

They know well that this young prodigy even consented to replace on certain occasions various conductors, so as the better to insure the success of a scheduled concert or performance. This brought honor and merit to the impresarios, but the name of the artist was guardedly kept in utter silence! The fact is they did not want to render homage to a man of color, for to do so would jeopardize the status of the race that governs our society. To recognize this artist would proclaim his superiority over others who, for fear of failing or of being criticized, did not dare even try to perform. He was one of the only two saxophonists then living in New Orleans. The public always relied on him heavily, but it seems that his solos were never perfect enough to make them forget the color of his skin. May we be permitted to relate here an incident that illustrates not only the egotism of prejudice, but also the smallness of certain natures.

A musician well known in this city had to return to New York on business. He asked our young artist to take care of this mission for him. It concerned submitting a composition to a renowned artist who would criticize the work. Our friend accepted the proposition. He made the trip to New York and was received by the artist with exquisite courtesy. In the course of the conversation, such criticisms as these came forth volubly: "This composition should be redone from the beginning to the end. Only the ballet needs no change *for it is perfect*. I will write a letter to my agent at New Orleans and give him all the neces-

A Tribute to the Creole People of Color

sary explanations. In this way you will not have to memorize all the details."

The young man was told the contents of the letter, which he dutifully brought to his employer, the supposed author of the musical composition. This man kept a grim silence about the contents of the message. The reason for this was that the "perfect ballet" was the creation of our young artist, and it would have done him too much honor to inform him of the decision of the man in New York. It was against the principles of Louisiana to let a man of color know that his work was better than that of a white man. If we keep secret the name of this musician, it is through respect for his grieving family who do not wish to be troubled during this period of sorrow and mourning.

This beloved son, whom nature was pleased to endow with talent that he was able to develop to the highest degree, has departed from our midst. But he has left behind a ray of sunlight that all earthly hatred can never extinguish. Heaven is more powerful than the obscurantism of this world. God has said, "Let there be light," and light was, and light will be, according to His holy and sovereign will.

Chapter VIII
Our Philanthropists of the Past ∽ How the Black Man Knows How to Give

OUR PHILANTHROPISTS OF THE PAST

Georges-Alcès
Here is a great-hearted man, one of those exceptional people who lived in the first half of the past century. In those days a person possessing his qualities was rare in our community. Mr. Georges-Alcès was one of the largest cigar manufacturers in New Orleans and he enjoyed a very lucrative and widespread business.[1] His success could be attributed to his integrity, industry, and knowledge of finance and commerce. This gentleman had in his employ throughout the year more than two hundred workers, all of them Creoles of color. He always paid them good wages and was ever concerned about their personal welfare. Those who worked in his factory had only to make known their needs, and he would provide for them at once without counting the cost. In a word his whole personnel constituted a family.

Georges-Alcès was a father to his compatriots. He was criticized and sometimes even vilified by certain jealous people, but like Augustus, he understood everything and he wanted to forget everything. This situation continued for several years. But there came a time when he had suffered so much ingratitude that no sensitive heart could remain indifferent. Patience ceased to be a virtue because the malicious attacks had exceeded their bounds.

1. Georges-Alcès inherited his place of business from his uncle, Lucien Mansion, great-grandfather of Charles Barthélemy Rousséve. Rousséve, *The Negro in Louisiana: Aspects of His History and His Literature* (New Orleans: Xavier University Press, 1937), 66.

A Tribute to the Creole People of Color

A certain Mr. C_____ opened a shop in competition with Mr. Georges-Alcès. This newcomer, no doubt finding that his business was not doing well enough, resolved to ruin his competitor. He wanted the patronage and prestige that Alcès enjoyed, and in his greed, throwing aside all decencies, he used the most despicable methods to gain his ends.

He began by hiring away his rival's employees. A good number of these disloyal workers accepted the offers that Mr. C_____ made them and went to work for him. These ingrates even organized into bands in order to take part in demonstrations to bring about the destruction of their former benefactor. Protestors paraded past his doors, howling, shrieking like wild beasts, repeating in chorus vile and obscene epithets against Alcès and his personnel.

It is unnecessary to add that most of these demonstrators were drunk. Moreover, it is said that they even carried out mock funeral processions under Mr. Alcès' balcony, accentuating their diabolical wish to do all possible harm to their former benefactor, this man who had given sustenance to more than fifty of the families represented in this horrible gang. Alcès recognized in the crowds familiar faces, people who still owed him large sums of money or who were obligated to him for favors they had received. This spectacle of ingratitude hurt Alcès cruelly. Brokenhearted, he determined to close his establishment so that he would no longer be the witness to or the victim of these shameful and criminal scenes. Some time after the Civil War, he left New Orleans to live in New York City. Ingratitude is known to breed the keenest bitterness. It is because of his ingratitude that the mayor of La Riole was stigmatized.

The actions of miserable people like those who betrayed, insulted, and persecuted Mr. Georges-Alcès, their friend, should be forever odious to us. Let us remember Georges-Alcès as a man of superior integrity, a person truly humane and worthy of the eulogies of a grateful posterity.

Our People and Our History

Thomy Lafon and Aristide Mary

Thomy Lafon and Aristide Mary were two well known and widely esteemed philanthropists. In life and in death, Lafon was exceedingly mindful of and generous to the underprivileged. In his will he left large donations to the poor; also he bequeathed a large sum for the construction of Berchmans Home. The Home for the Aged on Tonti Street and the Home for Boys on St. Peter Street were also built through his generosity, as was the Convent of the Holy Family. Thomy Lafon also contributed sizable sums to political movements that had as their end the defense of our rights. In all his philanthropy, he was never prompted by avarice or by self-gain. He donated only when he was convinced through proven truth that the cause was a worthy one. He was on his guard against abuse and pressure, but he never denied assistance to a worthy cause. Furthermore his philanthropy extended to all classes of society: the state, the Church, charitable organizations—all received testimony of his liberality, irrespective of race, color, sex, or age.

Although he was a Catholic, he was more interested in a poor person's problems than in his religion. He was as modest as he was generous, always wishing to maintain a silence about his good deeds. He was a true philanthropist.

Thomy Lafon was born in New Orleans of a French father and a Haitian mother.[2] His childhood was spent in poverty. In

---

2. A native of New Orleans, Lafon was born December 28, 1810, and died December 22, 1893; all authorities agree he was born a free person of color. Some historians believe he was the son of Pierre Laralde, who was either a Caucasian from France or a man of French extraction; his mother's family name was Foucher. Laralde may have deserted Lafon in his childhood; it is not known how he acquired the surname Lafon. Grace King, *New Orleans: The Place and the People* (New York: Macmillan Co., 1895), 352–53.

Newspapers attest that he was a philanthropist who gave to both races. He donated large sums to the American Anti-Slavery Society and to the underground railroad. Wilhelmena S. Robinson, *Historical Negro Biographies* (New York: Publishers Co., 1969), 92. At his death in 1893 he left the bulk of his fortune, about a half million dollars, to charity. Horace M. Bond, *The Education of the Negro in the American Social Order* (New York: Prentice-Hall, Inc., 1934), 145–46. He is thought to be the greatest Negro donor to education and to charity in the United States. A. E. Perkins (ed.), *Who's Who in Colored Louisiana* (Baton Rouge: Douglas Loan Co., Inc., 1930), 66. See also *Dictionary of American Biography*, s.v. Lafon, Thomy.

A Tribute to the Creole People of Color

growing up he became experienced in business; later in life he engaged in financial transactions. Through his innate talent for successful business dealings and through his extraordinary shrewdness, he soon accumulated extensive properties.

Lafon's fortune gave him so much prestige that, if he suffered from prejudice, it was only because of his sensitive and sympathetic personality. He always mingled with his own people. He was so respected in the business world that he was accorded a chair for his own use in each of the city's banks. This fact indeed speaks loudly for him. Lafon sought to avoid social gatherings so common in his day. He did this to such an extent that he was for a time regarded by unfeeling people as a callous miser. But this did not bother him and he never faltered in his pursuit of helping a good cause. Whenever he was approached in the interest of some charitable or patriotic work, the public could always count on his generosity. In cases of emergency, he would donate more than any other person. Everyone learned to recognize and appreciate Lafon by his good works. At his death the citizens of the city rendered the homage and tribute due him by perpetuating his name in several ways.

Aristide Mary, though less wealthy than Thomy Lafon, seemed to be even more generous than he. Lafon contributed in a methodical manner, whereas Mary gave without ever questioning. It is true the first donated more than the second, but he did so only when convinced of the worthiness of the cause. Mary lent his ear to every call: he extended his hand to everyone who asked. Like Lafon, Mary left memorials to charity in his last will. There is no exact estimate of the contributions of this man who never omitted giving to every cause, politics included. He believed in upholding our rights, the rights of all Louisianians, and he aided the cause with generous donations. For example, he would assume the responsibility for a lawsuit and would defray its expenses. He would go to the assistance of a family in distress whose needs had been made known to him. People said of him, "Mary always had his right hand in his pocket," signifying he never refused to give his money to a needy cause. He donated to the sick, the dead, the unfortunate, to every worthy need brought before him. He often told us that he did good for the love of good. And this was surely true. The proof of it is that despite the abuse and the ingratitude of his recipients, he continued to bestow his generous gifts to the end of his life. Thomy Lafon and Aristide Mary were two benefactors who deserve to be enshrined in our hearts along with Madame Bernard Couvent.

Julien Déjour

The subject of this story was an eminent, respectable man who rendered sovereign service to mankind through his works of charity. Julien Déjour was born at Cayes, Haiti, but we claim him as our own because he was reared by a Louisiana family, the Hermogène Raphael family that brought young Déjour to New Orleans and took care of him until he was grown. Déjour benefited from the kindnesses of Mr. Raphael, from whom he learned the trade of roofing with slate. He was a perfectionist in this trade, as some examples of his work testify to this day. But it is mainly because of the goodness of his heart that we wish here to record him among our compatriots. Because of the beauty of Julien Déjour's character, he was highly respected by his fellow men, by men in all walks of life.

There never existed a man more sensitive to the misfortunes of others. Almost every day of his life was marked by some act of kindness, which he made sure was kept hidden from the world. Truly, his left hand was ignorant of what his right hand did. This generous man created for himself an enviable position, but however much money he earned, he dispensed it to the needy and the poor. The white, the black, the yellow—all were the same in his eyes and all received from him equal compassion and monetary assistance. Such a man should not be forgotten. His memory should be kept alive among us as a touching memory. He deserves our sorrow and our praise, for he was good

A Tribute to the Creole People of Color

to the point of innocence, humane to the point of sacrifice. We should all hold dear Déjour's memory. He was born in 1850 and left this world in 1900; therefore, he was exactly fifty years old at his death.

Alcée Labat

Never did the Creoles of color boast a more loving and sympathetic man than Alcée Labat. This good man shared all the misfortunes of the Creole family—death, sickness, as well as the normal suffering which was so terrible and so common among us. His purse and his personal services were always at the disposal of the public. Labat gave much help to the poor, giving money whenever these unfortunate people found themselves in need. He gave this help without ostentation.

Both individuals and groups remember his good deeds; in fact, the name of Alcée Labat was known to everyone. All have respect for his character and for the generous way in which he distributed his good works.

Alcée Labat was a member of the Citizens' Committee and his associates will testify to his zeal and generosity in their cause. He signalized himself above all in relation to the legal proceedings that the committee undertook against the abuses of the 1890 legislature.

Until his death Labat retained the esteem and the respect of his people. He left several sons. They, like us, are justifiably proud of this man whose virtues and services should never be forgotten. People who knew him speak of his politeness as much as of his sensitivity. Never did an offensive word come from his lips. His manners were affable, his countenance was somewhat reserved but never disdainful. In every way Labat was a perfect gentleman. He was never known to betray his integrity. He was in truth jealous of his honor, eager to guard it. A slave to his promises, he fulfilled his every commitment. In the transaction of his business affairs, he took meticulous care always to be particularly honest.

Labat was one of the most influential supporters of *Le Crusader*, published here at the end of the last century.[3] His contributions to the maintenance of this paper were of great importance. His death was deeply regretted. This we can easily understand, for his presence among us meant a supporter for good causes, a friend for the poor, a defender for the oppressed.

---

3. See Chapter XII, below.

Chapter IX
The Creole Women of Color in the Catholic Churches ∾ The Generosity of Madame Bernard Couvent

THE CREOLE WOMEN OF COLOR

Most of the Creole women were exemplars of piety and charity. They were known to care for their own people. They never employed nurses for their sick, nor did they send their sick to hospitals. They took care of their own families and friends, helping them whenever they needed it.

At the beginning of the past century, the women of color were notably generous in their services to the Church. But, in time they were ostracized from the sanctuaries, and today there is hardly a pastor in the diocese who will admit that our women formerly gave their domestic services to the Church. There seems to be a silence about this matter. It is a known fact that several women even left their property to the Church, but these generous acts have been forgotten. We say this without bitterness. There was more than one Veronica in our colored population, and we had no beggars among us because the Creole women also made it a point to feed the poor. They tried to make the poor conscious of a certain degree of pride, and they encouraged them in the Christian faith, which they themselves professed with such fervor.

Kind, charitable, and pious, they thus took care of the bodies and souls of our poor people, exhorting them constantly to bear their lot with resignation. The Catholic religion had inculcated in them the principles of virtue, of love of God, and of neighborliness, principles that animated all their actions. It can be said in their praise that they cared for the sick with real skill, and the most fortunate results were often attributed to their indomitable vigilance.

Innumerable doctors appreciated and used their experience.

Our People and Our History

The men of science often deferred to the judgment of these noble women and followed their advice in cases known to be critical. Before the introduction of sanitary measures, such as exist today in our city, epidemics were frequent. They particularly attacked visitors to the city, whom they decimated rapidly. The lack of hospitals and the necessary equipment to care for patients augmented the seriousness of the situation, so that one was forced to depend on the charitable services of the women. These "nursing women," as they were called then, cared for the sick until they recovered or died. Sometimes they were paid for their services, but many times they gave their time, their vigilance, and their help for the love of God, without hope for recompense.

The Creole woman was as chaste and as pure in her hovel as was her more fortunate sister living in the midst of luxury. It was not necessary to give ostentatious proof of her character, so strongly imbued was she with religion and virtue. If there are minds today so vile as to try to blemish the memory of these noble women, seeking to lower them to the level of the brute, we will appeal the matter to the tribunal of history, which in all times and in all countries has vindicated the innocent.

The history of man and the Church will proclaim those facts that prejudice tried to enshroud in oblivion. The Creole woman knew how to study, to think, to pray. She was generous, helpful, and pious. Her virtue, her charity, and her devotedness could never be doubted. These virtues will always be her most beautiful ornaments.

A number of our girls, reared in the convents, became associates and members of the Order of the Sisters of Charity. Others became virtuous mothers of families that endowed Louisiana with that beautiful Creole race known for its talents. This race has furnished us inventors, sculptors, painters, poets, literary men, professors, merchants, planters, skilled artisans, all men of superior moral caliber. These excellent women therefore occupy a unique place in our traditions. Let us add that many famil-

A Tribute to the Creole People of Color

ies frequently confided to them the moral education of their children.

One of our most outstanding women was Miss Henriette Délile [sic].[1] This good person consecrated her whole life to the performance of good works. Pious like Madame Couvent, her thoughts were always concerned with the welfare of her fellow Creoles. Besides her cooperation in the establishment of several churches in New Orleans, Miss Délile was known for her constant ministrations to the needy and the suffering. She was the foundress of the Society of the Holy Family, of which order she was the first Mother Superior. When this society appealed to Mr. François Lacroix, this rich compatriot arranged the sale of a piece of land situated on St. Bernard Avenue, on which he built a magnificent edifice that was named *the Hospice of the Holy Family*. To this home the people confided their widows left without support and those women who wished to retire from the world in order to live in quiet retreat. The society became the nucleus of the Order of the Holy Family which today exists and which we all know so well. Thus the memory of Henriette Délile, the foundress, lives on . . . a woman who created the original group that dates back to 1840 or earlier.

Miss Henriette Délile, Madame Bernard Couvent, Madame François Lacroix were heads of charitable associations whose purposes were to provide food and lodging and to care for the needs of the Creole population, with no other motive than of loving their neighbors. Let us here recall the French poet and hope that, "the echoes will not have forgotten these *great* names." Miss Henriette Délile died November 17, 1862, at the age of fifty.

1. The Congregation of the Sisters of the Holy Family was established in 1842 in New Orleans by Henriette Delisle and Juliette Gaudin, two young women of color, assisted by Marie Aliquot, a young French woman. The congregation conducted schools in the city and in other parts of the United States, as well as in Latin America. The sisters maintain homes for orphans and for the aged. Their present motherhouse is located in New Orleans. Charles Barthélemy Rousséve. *The Negro in New Orleans* (New Orleans: Archives of Negro History, Inc., 1969), 6.

Our People and Our History

Madame Louisa R. Lamotte

Madame Louisa Lamotte is one of our literary lights. This woman was well known for her erudition and for the great services that she rendered to the cause of education. She won high commendation as directress of the College of Young Women at Abbeville, France, in which country she taught for forty years. Some years before her death, she received from the French government the award of the *Palmes Académiques*.[2] That she was so honored by France and by the learned societies of Europe is worthy of consideration indeed. This fact alone offers sufficient testimony to her remarkable deeds and her claim to fame.

The leaders of France were not alone in expressing appreciaiton for her merits. *L'Abeille* of New Orleans to which Madame Lamotte contributed expressed profound regrets at her death in 1907. A memento from this newspaper follows here:

Memento

We learn, not without being deeply saddened, of the death of a woman whom we held in the most respectful esteem, a woman who has long honored us with her written contributions and who for many months had been held captive in her home by ill health—Madame Louisa Lamotte. We do not know the details that surrounded the death of this noble woman, but we have every assurance she had no fear of death, for her conscience was always calm and serene. Madame Lamotte was born in New Orleans, but she was reared in France, where she spent most of her life. She came to New Orleans because of the attractions our city held for her, and she labored here in full dedication until she exhausted her strength.

In Paris Madame Lamotte conducted a school for young girls. She founded in that city a literary magazine, *Revue*, which she edited most successfully. The government recognized her merit and awarded her the *Palmes Académiques*. Never in all her contacts was she known to

2. Louisa R. Lamotte, born in New Orleans, was reared and educated in France. She received the Palms (for academic merit) of the French Academy in 1881, sponsored a literary publication in Paris, and was the author of a number of books. Edward Larocque Tinker, *Les écrits de langue française en Louisiane au XIXe siècle* (Paris: Libraire Ancienne Honoré Champion, 1932), 271; Paul Harvey and Janet Heseltine (eds.), *The Oxford Companion to French Literature* (Oxford: Clarendon Press, 1959), 534.

A Tribute to the Creole People of Color

parade her wealth of knowledge or her superior degree of learning. She was too modest and humble for that. She was a kind, virtuous woman.

Her keenest desire was to return to France to resume relations so long interrupted and to see again her only living relative, her daughter. She died with this desire. We know this sweet dream will become a reality in the Great Beyond where the just are rewarded for their good deeds.

Virginie Girodeau

Much is said of Virginie Girodeau but we lack positive information relative to her. All we know is that she performed on the stage during the time of Armand Lanusse and Edmond Orso. We know too that she excelled in tragic drama. But nothing is recorded of her childhood or of her early education. It is believed that Miss Virginie perfected herself in her art under the direction of Mr. Perennès, the celebrated French professor of the past century.

In any case, she left an enviable reputation as a tragedienne. The fact that the public gave her a unique place in the history of amateur theater is ample commendation. She excelled in the theater of the Renaissance. For this reason she had the right to see her name destined for posterity and surrounded with all the respect due her merit. Since the purpose of this book is to set forth the qualities and virtues by which our small population distinguished itself, especially during the time of slavery, one small sketch, if it is well drawn, will find a place here. That is why we place Madame Virginie Girodeau among our prominent personalities whose glory deserves to be remembered. We would be forgetful of our duty should we fail to do so.

Madame the Widow, Bernard Couvent

Madame Couvent, a black African woman, was perhaps a slave in her youth.[3] She lived in New Orleans and left a legacy that

---

3. Justine Fervin Couvent, widow of Gabriel Bernard Couvent and a free woman of color, was at one time a slave in New Orleans. She died at eighty on June 28, 1837, leaving property in land and several houses to found a school for poor black Catholic orphans of the Third District. Charles

has produced inestimable results. Madame Couvent's generosity must have attracted wide attention. There would be reason then for being astonished if any of her contemporaries failed to record her name in history. It is an undeniable fact that she was the first among us to give the example of enlightened charity, and for a long time she was the only one who held this distinction. Her attitude on the question of education has been a genuine reproach to the wealthy people of her era. We have very little information about Madame Couvent. People often spoke of this aged lady. They extolled her piety and her charity, but nothing is known of her birth. It is believed she was born in Africa.

About the year 1832, this Christian woman left through her will several small houses for founding a school for indigent Catholic orphans of the Third District. It seems that she died about the year 1836, but her last testament relative to her bequest to the orphans was not executed until 1848, twelve years later. A society created at this time called for an account from the executor of the will concerning the misuse of the properties

---

Barthélemy Roussève, *The Negro in Louisiana: Aspects of His History and His Literature* (New Orleans: Xavier University Press, 1937), 43-44. The school, a coeducational, non-sectarian day school conducted separate classes for boys and girls; instruction was given in French and English. Parents who were able paid a monthly tuition; the orphanage received grants from wealthy free blacks and occasional small appropriations from the state. The school's principal benefactors were Thomy Lafon and Aristide Mary. Betty Porter, "The History of Negro Education in Louisiana," *Louisiana Historical Quarterly*, XXV (July, 1942), 278.

A booklet of twenty-eight pages, *History of the Catholic Indigent Orphans' Institute*, probably published in 1916 or 1917 (it is unpaged and undated), indicates that from the school's earliest days the free blacks were supporters of the institute. Names listed include Roussève, Lafon, Lanusse, Cohen, Joubert, Doyle, Lacroix, Desdunes, Artistide Mary, Estèves, Boise, Trévigne, and Martinet. The two Desdunes listed in the booklet are under the heading "Names of Directors from 1840 to 1915." Under another heading, "Names of Professors and Teachers, 1840-1915," appears another Desdunes, probably Rodolphe, for it carries the initials R. L. His brother, P. A. Desdunes, is likewise listed here.

The school, sponsored by the Catholic Society for the Instruction of Indigent Orphans, was duly incorporated according to state law. Now named Holy Redeemer School, it is located on Dauphine Street and is staffed by the Sister Servants of the Holy Ghost and Mary Immaculate. Porter, "The History of Negro Education," 278.

involved. Restitution was duly made and a settlement provided for the establishment of a primary school for black orphans of the Third District. One portion of the bequeathed property was located at the corner of Union and Grands Hommes [Great Men] streets. There for the first time classroom instruction was given, under the auspices of a Bureau of Directors that was organized to see that the wishes of Madame Couvent were fulfilled.

Madame Couvent stated in her will that the school should be placed under the supervision of the Catholic clergy. In virtue of this particular clause, Father Manehault, Madame Couvent's spiritual director, busied himself with the particulars of her legacy and assumed the duty of preserving it for the benefit of the orphans.[4] This good priest, being aware of negligence in the execution of the will, decided to intervene. His first step was to solicit the interest of Mr. François Lacroix, a man of eccentric character, but with a great heart. With no loss of time, Mr. Lacroix obtained the help of friends. Through donations,

---

4. Constantine Manehault was stationed at St. Louis Cathedral at various times from 1842 to 1864. *Register,* St. Louis Cathedral, New Orleans.

In the Faubourg Marigny lived two free families of color, the Fletchers and the Couvents. Both Couvent and Fletcher were carpenters and their families worshipped at the Cathedral. Couvent and his wife, Justine Fervin, had amassed quite a modest sum of money, and her one dream, as she grew older, was to provide a school for orphans of the free people of color, many of whom had white fathers. She herself had had no formal education. The Couvents had no children, and when Bernard Couvent died, May 22, 1829, at seventy-one, he left his entire estate to his widow.

Her religious director, and a lifelong friend of her husband's friend Henry Fletcher, was Father Manehault; it was he who encouraged and directed the widow in the disposal of her property for this purpose. Her will was drawn up in 1832, naming Fletcher executor and Manehault, or his successor, supervisor. When she died eight years following her husband's death, there arose a problem involved in establishing the school. The difficulty centered in the category of the school, for although private schools existed for whites and for blacks, nonmixed and sometimes mixed, education by and through an established institution for free people of color was not favored by city authorities, even when under the auspices of the community's leading Catholic church.

Because of the objections, for almost a dozen years, the will was inoperative, until a voluntary corporation, organized for the purpose of implementing the document, succeeded in their legal action. Marcus Christian, *Dream of an African Ex-Slave* (New Orleans: Louisiana Weekly Publishing Co., 1938), 8, courtesy of Tulane University Library, Special Collections, Louisiana Division.

fairs, and the like, these men not only obtained funds to clear the titles of the properties, but they even bought other land to augment Madame Couvent's estate.

They erected a fine building and established a coeducational school with pupils coming from all sections of the city.[5] It was presided over by five or six instructors, teaching both in French and English. Félicie Cailloux was the first teacher [and first principal] in the Madame Couvent school. She was a black woman, exceedingly intelligent, highly respected, a devout Catholic. After her tenure a change was made in the location and size of the school. Among the principals were listed Lanusse, Lavigne, Snaër, Questy, Christopher, Reynès, Lainez, Sent-Manat, Camps, Vigers, Duhart, Trévigne, Madames Thézan and Populus, and others whose names escape us.

Later on Lafon, Mary, and several other benefactors added to the properties left by Madame Couvent. François Lacroix and his co-workers also made contributions to the institute.

During several years before the war of 1861, the directors sometimes obtained gifts from the state legislature and from the city of New Orleans. The importance of this institute is the fact that it was the best attended school during the time of slavery. All the teachers were of the black race; thus they were able to develop sympathetic relationships with the children in their care. The pupils received a well-rounded education, intellectually, morally, physically, and spiritually.

Madame Couvent herself had had no formal education, but she is said to have been blessed with a wealth of common sense. She had a deep compassion for little children condemned to live without the advantages of education in the midst of so much indifference and even hostility toward a class of people sorely tried. Guided, no doubt, by the counsel of her spiritual director, Father Manehault, she did not hesitate to place all her worldly goods at the disposal of the unfortunate for the sole purpose of

5. In 1850 almost 80 percent of the city's free people of color were literate and more than a thousand of their children attended school. Finnian P. Leavens, "*L'Union* and the New Orleans *Tribune* and Louisiana Reconstruction" (M.A. thesis, Louisiana State University, 1966), 3–4.

A Tribute to the Creole People of Color

saving them from ignorance. These generous donations by Madame Couvent were made during the difficult times of slavery. It was a grave error on the part of her contemporaries to have neglected transmitting to us the precise details in the life story of this generous person.

In 1848 Father Manehault took upon himself the task of directing her, and introducing her to other people interested in education. Madame Couvent must have been a very pious and a deeply respected person, because Father Manehault recommended her to his friends. Thanks to the inexhaustible solicitude of this priest, she was finally recognized and her legacy handled properly and made applicable to its original purposes.

It is proper to mention these facts not only for the sake of history, but also for reasons of paying due tribute to the good will, to the charity of this holy man who did so much to honor the Catholic Church. Without the help of this servant of God, the people would have been left in complete ignorance of this great woman. He told who she was, what she did, and the manner of life she lived. The presence of Madame Couvent brought to the Creole population a succession of intellectual and moral developments which flowered under the direction of capable teachers. We will not say that writers during the lifetime of Madame Couvent neglected her. We know that during her era it was difficult to have manuscripts published. It was difficult to place notices in newspapers. It is understandable therefore how our compatriots seemingly overlooked this good woman as well as other distinguished people of her day. Everything in those days was done by small groups. People with the same vocations or with the same interests gathered in private groups, where only their own particular interests were considered. We are happy to state that numerous writers, poets, artists, who displayed exemplary conduct and superior intellects went forth from the doors of the institute for indigent orphans.

They say it is necessary to go back to the source of things. In conformity with this principle, all the benefits that the Creole people received from this school for the poor were due to the

Our People and Our History

generosity of this African woman: the widow Madame Bernard Couvent.

Before her time there were schools in our city, but poor people were unable to attend them.[6] At the institute founded by this charitable woman, the children were charged only a very modest tuition, and orphans were admitted free of charge. The monthly fee never rose above fifty sous. For this modest sum of half a dollar a month, often the child was given not only his instruction but the use of textbooks which the school furnished when parents were unable to provide them.

It is of interest to know that every year on the feast of All Saints the directors held a school funds drive. They did this by placing at the gate of the cemetery two trays to receive offerings. The trays were supervised by orphans chosen by the directors. There were times when the donations were most substantial. They were used for the various operating costs of the school. Also, it was a custom each year to have a Mass said for the repose of the soul of the good widow, Madame Couvent. The upkeep of her tomb, located in the last cemetery on Claiborne Avenue, was paid for by the board of directors. In the latter years, the board placed a commemorative plaque in the school to honor the foundress of the institute. We believe it is the duty of the Creole people of color to erect a larger monument to the memory of this noble woman. We believe, too, we should remember the

---

6. Before Reconstruction, blacks in New Orleans were educated in private schools or by private tutors. The wealthy people of color sent their children to Europe or to New England for their education. In the first years following its establishment in 1827, the Ursulines' school accepted whites, Indians, Negro slaves, and free people of color, both resident and day pupils. Negroes were excluded from the New Orleans public school established in 1841, although blacks were taxed like other citizens in the support of education. In 1860 the city's Negroes owned a fifth of the taxable property, their holdings estimated at $22,000,000.

In addition to the Couvent school, and later the Sisters of the Holy Family school, there was the Nelson Medard school, which was attended by black and white pupils. Other smaller schools were privately maintained. After the Civil War, several educational institutions for blacks opened in New Orleans. Among these were Straight University (preparatory and normal), Leland University, and Southern University (as well as Southern University in Baton Rouge). Rousséve, *The Negro in New Orleans*, 5-6.

A Tribute to the Creole People of Color

dead through memorial societies. It is our duty to recognize justice in regard to departed benefactors. Today, with a number of philanthropists in our midst, we could interest them in forming such a group in memory of Madame Couvent. May the future generations not reproach us for our neglect in this matter, especially when the spirit of the times exhorts us to glorify the good deeds accomplished by her gifts. Yes, the names of the widow Madame Bernard Couvent, of Thomy Lafon, of Aristide Mary should be ever honored by us! Their names should be kept before our people through appropriate evidence of our love and gratitude for the magnanimous contributions they made to us!

With the Civil War and its aftermath, matters changed. During the period of Reconstruction, most of the children of color attended the public free schools along with the white children. The Couvent institute therefore became almost deserted: in 1884 the school was almost in ruins. Poor administration for several years was partly to blame for the decline of the institute. Whatever was the case, some patriots united their efforts to restore the school to its former prestige. The task was indeed a difficult one but the valiant supporters once again came to the fore. The following twelve patriotic and generous men were chiefly instrumental in this project: Arthur Estèves, Eugène Luscy, Noël Bacchus, Nelson Fouché, Armand Duhart, J. S. Gautier, P. A. Desdunes [brother of Rodolphe Desdunes],[7] Donatien Déruisé, Charles Charbonnet, Philip Michel, Clovis Gallaud, and R. L. Desdunes. Nine of these men who formed the board of directors in 1884 are now dead. Through their devoted leadership, the Creoles rallied to the cause and inaugurated a new era of prosperity and independence for the venerable school.

7. P. A. Desdunes' writings are indicative of an excellent education. He seems to have had a "spiritually sensitive nature" that easily detected injustice. Although, like most Creoles, he held for the Catholic Church the highest respect, he was not unaware of its shortcomings. Patriotism was for him the highest and strongest of human sentiments and he was strongly civic-minded. He served on the board of directors of the Couvent Institute. Edward Maceo Coleman, *Creole Voices: Poems in French by Free Men of Color* (Washington, D.C.: The Associated Publishers, Inc., 1945), xxv.

Our People and Our History

There was question for a while of converting the place into a convent. The Catholic clergy deemed this expedient because the school had long since changed its methods of teaching and thus no longer fulfilled the wishes of Madame Couvent. However, Archbishop Le Ray acceded to the decisions of the board of directors, whose authority he respected.[8] Today the institute for indigent orphans is reorganized, it has received new help, and the Creole population seems to have renewed its attachment to the school. Let us hope our people will ever more and more appreciate the foresight and the charity of Madame Bernard Couvent. She was the first person to bring decent living and the opportunity for learning into the lives of our black orphans.

---

8 Francis Xavier Le Ray, archbishop of New Orleans, was born near Rennes, France, in 1825. He came to the United States in 1843 and was appointed in 1877 by Pius IX as successor to Bishop August M. Martin of Natchitoches, Louisiana. Roger Baudier, *The Catholic Church in Louisiana* (New Orleans: A. W. Hyatt Co., 1939), 439.

Chapter X
The Emigration of 1858 ∽ The Politics of the Emperor Faustin I of Haiti ∽ Two Great Figures: Emile Desdunes and Captain Octave Rey

THE EMIGRATION OF 1858

The laws of 1855 were excessively severe on the free population of color, in spite of the fact our people enjoyed a distinguished ancestry, material wealth, education, and respectability, as testified later by Mr. Canonge himself.[1]

From the very beginning it was forbidden for persons of color to trace their origin; this prohibition was a natural consequence of the law which forbade civil marriage between a person of color and one of the white race. Nevertheless, white persons of Latin extraction, more conscientious of morals and word of honor, contracted religious marriages and thus avoided the stigma of prostitution. Therefore, if our ancestors before the war had not the right of succession, at least they bore the name of their parents, their fathers and their mothers, and were admitted to the sacraments of the Catholic religion.[2] It is correct

---

1. Louis Placide Canonge (1822-93) was a Creole of color. He was a professor in New Orleans; he contributed to *L'Abeille* and directed the *Courrier français*. Edward Larocque Tinker, *Les écrits de langue française en Louisiane au XIX° siècle* (Paris: Libraire Ancienne Honore Champion, 1932), 66.
Canonge has been described as a white journalist who wrote for *L'Abeille*. Finnian P. Leavens, "*L'Union* and the New Orleans *Tribune* and Louisiana Reconstruction" (M.A. thesis, Louisiana State University, 1966), 20.
See also Grace King, *Creole Families of New Orleans* (New York: Macmillan Co., 1921), 393, 395.

2. "It is true, the free Negro's position in the South was precarious, occupying a sort of uncertain and undefined position in our midst. His color suggested servitude, but his status secured a portion of freedom. . . . He suffered many of the inhibitions of his slave brothers, while enjoying some privileges denied them. His advantages, however, were: he could marry, have children, and enjoy something of a normal family life. He could own property, have the right to his earnings, and engage in a few trades forbidden the enslaved. . . . There was at least a measure of independence and in the privacy of the home could be found a seclusion from the constant surveillance of the white world. . . . In the streets the distinction among black

to maintain that there were always upright people among us. Without their presence, without their intervention, the position of honorable men would have become a source of intolerable torture.

Among the stringent regulations imposed upon the people of color was the stipulation that they be represented by a white agent in all civil transactions, such as contracts of sale, of purchase, and the like. As one may surmise, such a ruling favoring the interests of the oppressor was readily endorsed by a large section of the public, who supported it warmly.

The press united with the legislators, and it seemed for a time that the ultimate sentence would be pronounced against the victims by the new despotism. One can appreciate the intervention of the noble and gracious citizens we have referred to, and others like Mr. Sigure, who opposed this act with all their strength and resources. Mr. Sigure succeeded in getting an indefinite postponement of this matter bearing on our lives. It is to the intervention of this noble citizen and his friends that the free men of 1855 are indebted for being saved from this infamy that threatened to abolish all their personal rights. With the advent of the war, our cause was aided again, for it brought focus to bear on the hostilities our people were facing at this time. We were not far removed from the status of slavery.

A free person of color was forbidden to walk the streets without a permit; a black visitor to the city could not remain in New Orleans without the guarantee or protection of a white person; a black man could not defend his honor nor that of his family with any assurance of justice. Any statement considered as seditious cost him the privilege of remaining in the city and sentenced him to several years of enforced labor. Any free black man who possessed wealth and the respect of his peers was the sure target of arrest, ill treatment, and imprisonment, according

---

people was not clear. In the court the free were sometimes only fined, while slaves were whipped; legislation increasingly covered all blacks with only nominal regard for status." Allen Weinstein and Frank Otto Gatell (eds.), *American Negro Slavery: A Modern Reader* (New York: Oxford University Press, 1968), 102.

A Tribute to the Creole People of Color

to the caprice of the most depraved police officers or of denunciation by the most despicable residents of the city. Violence became more manifest and more common in New Orleans each day.[3]

Hate was added to prejudice. This was true particularly among the younger generation, which undoubtedly was preparing for the crisis of 1860. The agitation of Garrison, the speeches of Sumner, of Lincoln, the actions of John Brown in Kansas against the extension of slavery had fired minds and hearts so that the people of New Orleans succumbed to the same pressures that were afflicting the South elsewhere. Avarice was the source of all the trouble. Slavery paid. Slavery must be saved at any price!

It must be noted here that foreigners and newcomers to New Orleans from faraway shores after 1840 were not of the same mentality as the earlier people, who came from chivalric origins and who preserved the ideals of their class. The newcomers were mere adventurers, attracted to the city solely by the lure of gain, with one purpose in mind, namely, exploitation and profit. They utilized slavery as their main source of revenue. Every enterprise, every transaction revolved around slavery: business, politics, and even religion.

These strangers to our city became powerful through their numbers and their common interests. They became either slaveowners or aspired toward ownership. Their ranks quickly grew strong, so that by 1852–1853, thanks to the support given them by certain Louisianians, they had acquired a dominant influence in the community. The greater the success of these adventurers, the more that "divine institution," as slavery was then called, became oppressive. Prejudice now made itself felt against our free people of color in new ways. The newcomers were most

---

3. In addition death was the penalty for a free person of color (or a slave) who willfully burned or destroyed any building, house, grain, and so forth. A fine and imprisonment was the penalty for insulting or assaulting and beating any white person, for betting, for gambling with a slave or for harboring a runaway slave, and for entering the state without a proper legal permit. Ulrich B. Phillips, *Revised Statutes of Louisiana* (New Orleans: John Claiborne, 1856), Black Code, Sections 8, 12, 15, 51, 94, 99.

domineering, overbearing, and cruel. And Bernard de Marigny's protégés of 1845, who held the leadership, had no limit to their ambitions, while the free people of color were suspect because of their sympathy for the slaves, even though there were no exterior signs of this feeling.[4]

The newcomers believed it was necessary to reduce our people to powerlessness either through intimidation or through exile. Ordinary restrictions no longer sufficed. They would make slaves of us also. To this end the new leaders addressed themselves to the legislature, and they obtained laws that threatened further danger to the freedom and rights of our people, even to ejection from the state. In this impasse some of our people chose to exile themselves to Haiti.[5]

Emile Desdunes

In 1858 Emile Desdunes was the New Orleans representative agent for emigration. He received this position through the authority of Emperor Faustin I Soulouque of Haiti. His business was to arrange the expatriation of all Creoles of color who wished to leave the city. The fact that the New Orleans city authorities offered no objection to his mission, despite the law

4. Bernard Marigny (de Marigny de Mandeville) was born in New Orleans in 1785 and was educated in France. He was the son of a distinguished family and for a time was very wealthy. Alcée Fortier, *A History of Louisiana* (4 vols.; New York: Manzi, Joyant and Co., 1904), I, pt. 1, p. 171. Marigny inherited from his father a large estate that lay "just below the lower line of the city—where Elysian Fields Avenue ran northwest from the river." John Smith Kendall, *History of New Orleans* (3 vols.; Chicago: Lewis Publishing Co., 1922), I, 125. In 1808, when he was twenty, Marigny sold a part of his plantation, which was subdivided into lots and developed into the Faubourg Marigny. In addition to his planting and speculative activities, Marigny was active as a local and state politician. He was a Democrat in the 1830's, but became a Native American leader in the 1850's. John G. Clark, *New Orleans, 1718–1812: An Economic History* (Baton Rouge: Louisiana State University Press, 1970), 277n2.

5. In 1860 there were 23,974 Negroes in New Orleans; 10,689 free and 13,285 slaves, in a total population of 168,675. Roland Wingfield, "The Creoles of Color: A Study of a New Orleans Subculture" (M.A. thesis, Louisiana State University, 1961), 36–37. The New Orleans *Daily Delta* reported in 1860 the exodus of free persons for Mexico and Haiti. Donald E. Everett, "Free Persons of Color in New Orleans, 1803–1865" (Ph.D. dissertation, Tulane University, 1952), 129, citing New Orleans *Delta*, January 15, 1860.

A Tribute to the Creole People of Color

against it, is sufficient proof that the procedure was agreeable to the slave owners.

It seems that Emperor Soulouque, acting on the basis of reports that he had received, decided to send Emile Desdunes to New Orleans to inquire into the condition and opinion of all people of Haitian descent. Emile Desdunes was an educated man, honest and energetic. Because he had been born in New Orleans and was Haitian by education and custom, Emperor Soulouque judged him to be thoroughly capable of carrying out his project.[6] Desdunes justified all his expectations. His remarkable ability and sincerity produced an excellent impression from the moment of his arrival in the city. With the confidence and respect of the good Creole families assured him he succeeded at once in his first efforts. But this success proved to be only short-lived.

The revolution led by General [Fabre] Geffrard overthrew Soulouque's government. Geffrard and the new leaders were less interested in the fate of Louisianians seeking exile in Haiti. The result was that the emigration movement ceased. Colonel Desdunes retired, and shortly afterward all communication between Haiti and New Orleans came to a complete halt.

Emile Desdunes died at Port-au-Prince about the year 1862 and since then there has never been further question about emigration between Louisiana and the country of Dessalines.[7] It is unfortunate that the people did not judge it expedient to

6. Soulouque was an illiterate former slave who is said to have misruled Haiti for twelve years (1847–59) in *opera-buffe* style, crowning himself emperor in 1849. History records that he persecuted the mulatto bourgeoisie mercilessly. He was succeeded by Fabre Geffrard, who is considered to have been a good president. Roland C. Wingfield, "Haiti: A Case Study of an Underdeveloped Area" (Ph.D. dissertation, Louisiana State University, 1966), 41–42.

7. In 1802 General Jean Jacques Dessalines led a successful revolt in Saint-Domingue against the French and restored the colony's original Indian name, Haiti. During the revolt many French colonials were massacred. He proclaimed Haitian independence, January 1, 1804; one month later he ordered and had carried out the killing of almost all of the French residents—priests, doctors, and other "useful" citizens were spared. Dessalines was assassinated in 1806. The exodus of French colonials, which began in 1791 and climaxed in 1802, brought about 10,000 planters, *gens de couleur*, and their respective slaves to New Orleans. *Ibid.*, 35–40.

Our People and Our History

keep a door open for foreign travel, because there are times in the life of a suffering people when it is good to have a change of climate. The man of color can, without appearing ridiculous, entertain ideas of exchanging residence to relieve his circumstances just as other human beings do. The love of self, the love of one's family, and of his fellow men should be as strong as the love of one's country.

Captain Octave Rey

This gentleman was one of the best-known citizens of our city and one of the most highly esteemed and respected. He descended from one of the old families of New Orleans. [Born in 1837], he was the son of Mr. Barthélemy Rey, a member of the first school board of the institute for indigent orphans. [He died in 1908.] His brothers were Hippolyte and Henry L. Rey, both worthy men who zealously occupied themselves with the fate of their people.

Henry and Hippolyte Rey served competently as officers during the War of Secession. Octave, the youngest of the Rey brothers, was a tall man of herculean proportions—energetic, powerful, and dynamic in his thinking. Everyone knew Octave Rey. Everyone respected him for his tremendous courage and his strong determination. At the expiration of his military service in the Civil War, he became immersed in the political affairs of his time and he won praise as a Republican leader. He served with the rank of captain with the Metropolitan Police, meriting a high rating with his superiors.[8]

Captain Rey made some very important arrests, which were often performed under the most perilous circumstances. He was observed at every scene of danger, leading his men into action. He was captain on the police force from 1868 to 1877, that is, from the beginning of the administration of Governor War-

---

8. Edwin L. Jewell (ed.), *Jewell's Crescent City Illustrated* (New Orleans: n.p., 1873), Appendix VII, lists Rey as a member of the Metropolitan Police, Fourth Precinct.

A Tribute to the Creole People of Color

moth to that of Governor [Stephen B.] Packard, who decided to give up his post and was sent as consul to Liverpool.[9]

One can easily say that Packard's departure marked the end of Reconstruction, for Louisiana a period of bloody debacle. New Orleans particularly was the theater of riots, assassinations, and violence of all kinds. The people lived in constant fear and terror. While the press condemned all such actions, secret societies were plotting and orators were adding to the disorders with their passionate, fiery harangues. The Church, the courts, every profession contributed to the agitation. It was an open conviction that the man of color was the target of the onslaught. No one was spared in this public outburst. Federal officials themselves were in danger of their lives.

Thus it was that Mr. Joseph Soudé, a man of color, was assassinated on *La Levee*. He was a Customhouse officer, the first man of the black race to be employed under the national administration. The crime was never punished. At this time, to kill a black man or to kill a Republican regardless of his color was considered a commendable and patriotic thing to do. Captain Rey was in the middle of all this turmoil. The bands of hostile, armed men who prowled the streets classed themselves as avengers. They were inspired by the hatred that aroused the old citizens against the new black ones and against the white men who were charged with seeing that the principles of Reconstruction were respected.

A particular animosity was directed against the Metropolitan police. The aggressive part of the city's population looked on the police as the chief tool of the new regime and thus as a serious obstacle to their own ambitions. Nocturnal attacks, assaults of every description, and deaths were frequent. The sentry officers

---

9. Henry Clay Warmouth (1842–1931) was a Union soldier from Illinois. In 1865 he opened a law office in New Orleans and in November of that year, he was elected "territorial delegate" to Congress by Louisiana Unionists but was denied a seat. He was elected governor of Louisiana in 1868, with Negro Oscar J. Dunn as lieutenant governor. *Dictionary of American Biography*, s.v. Warmoth, Henry Clay.

were chased from their posts and sometimes killed on the spot. It was a common thing to recall these unfortunate policemen to their guardhouse in order to save them from a sudden attack or even certain death. Assassination was the order of the day. The Republican authorities wished to avoid conflict and endeavored to appease the minds of the enraged people rather than reproach them for having excited their passions.

Moderation was the policy of the party in power and it was only on occasions of extreme provocation that it used force to put down violence. The riot of September 14, 1874, was the only occasion when the government tried to maintain its authority with the use of arms. In all other cases, the [Republican] administration was wise and conciliating in an effort to avoid bloodshed and in the hope of seeing its powers strengthened through the use of peaceful methods. But all these concessions were made in vain. The people involved in this crisis had created a problem whose solution would come only through a change of government such as they had planned.[10]

It was evident that the violence used was meant to destroy or to lessen the power of constituted authority. It was in the midst of these upheavals against the established laws that Captain Rey demonstrated his nobility and courage. He exerted to full capacity his sound judgment, his astute mind. He never failed to do his duty despite the difficulties that surrounded him. He was not a highly educated man, but he was just toward everyone, regardless of race or political persuasion. Brave and generous, his conduct was ever in conformity with his duty and his dignity as an officer of the law. He was one of those men who could face the most difficult challenge and prove himself equal to the most delicate responsibility. He possessed a prodigious memory for names and people. He could call out the name of almost all the residents of the city and he knew them at sight. This facility that he had of remembering people, the location

---

10. For a discussion of Radical politics and the disputed election of 1874, see E. Merton Coulter, *The South During Reconstruction, 1865–1877* (Baton Rouge: Louisiana State University Press, 1947), 352–53.

A Tribute to the Creole People of Color

of places and events made him a unique character in the community.

Always understanding and sympathetic, Rey was the confidant of the people. He served as arbiter in all affairs that concerned the reconciliation of opposing sides. People trusted his good common sense, his impartiality, and his qualities as a gentleman. Octave Rey had the honor of representing his district as state senator. His death in October, 1908, caused as much surprise as regret, for nothing had indicated his end was near. The newspapers published articles about him and spoke of him at length with the highest eulogies. His funeral was elaborate. People from all sections of the city flocked to the services. This in itself was significant proof of his popularity. The mortal remains of this great captain repose in the cemetery on Bienville Street in the family tomb.

Four sons and one daughter, highly esteemed children, survive him. People spoke of Captain Rey long after his death. He was praised as one of those exceptional men whose personality lives in the memory of his fellow men. His death was an irreparable loss. Assuredly Captain Rey was a superior man, superior in intelligence, superior in will power, superior in patriotism. Had he lived in a society less biased against people of color, he would have shone in its highest ranks. It was not an easy task to have to fight against a population guided exclusively by prejudice. No one knew this better than Captain Rey, but he never ceased to fight until the very end. He cherished all through his noble and active life the principle, "Equal opportunities for all men."

The Creole people of color for whom he fought and suffered will not fail to honor him for his merits. Deprived of the liberty to conduct his patriotic enterprises, he succumbed under the weight of his opposition. His lack of success does not indicate physical cowardice or moral weakness, for the captain could say, as in Racine's tragedy, "I fear God . . . no one else." All those who knew him understood this. He may be compared with the celebrated Jean Fléming, a wealthy resident of color, who in

1836 was commissioned to carry a petition to the speaker of the house. We are quite sure that this petition, however respectful in its text, must have contained an expression of some sore grievance. The act of presenting this document in the name of black persons was in itself a bold step that could have cost Fléming's life, but he was dauntless. He would not be deterred from his mission. Similarly Captain Rey often exposed his life to grave dangers in constituting himself the agent of his compatriots in the most critical circumstances. Like Jean Fléming, he was determined. He lived according to his motto, "I will do my duty come what may!"

Rey had a certain stoic attitude inherited from his ancestors, who had not only showed constancy and fortitude in their misfortunes, but had even manifested disdain for any and all threats. There once occurred in his life a very interesting incident which belongs to this part of our history.

In 1862, at the time of the seizure of New Orleans by Union troops and Admiral Farragut's sailors, General Butler issued a proclamation ordering all the citizens to surrender their arms. Now, the weapons of the Confederate regiment of color were in the hands of several officers of this corps. These men had taken the precaution of hiding the arms in various safe places. One allotment was hidden in the *Salle d'Economie*, another in Claiborne Hall, and still another in the orphans' [Couvent] school. Heeding the order of the commander, a group of officers in charge of these arms decided to report their location to Butler and learn his exact wishes regarding disarmament in the city. The committee charged with this mission was composed of four men: Henry L. Rey, Edgar Davis, Eugène Rapp, and Octave Rey. Here begins the history of the first black regiment in the Union army. These men were the representatives of the Creole people of color, and they were the first to give the example of loyalty to the cause of the Union. There are other persons who claim this honor, but knowing the conditions that existed in 1862, it is necessary to reject the pretense that every man of color stepped forward who was not a slave at the time.

A Tribute to the Creole People of Color

General Butler, no doubt, perceiving that his visitors were men of intelligence, of civic responsibility, and of education, spoke with them on this question, which was of more importance than was the delivery of some old rifles that they said were quite useless long before they had been issued to the soldiers. After having heard their report, he asked, "What are the feelings of your people in regard to the federal government?" Then he added, "Do not hurry. Leave and think seriously on the reply that you will formulate for me."

Following the general's advice, these men went to a private place to consult among themselves in order to be better prepared to assume the responsibility of their declaration. Henry L. Rey took the answer to General Butler saying that they had not held an assembly of the people to discover exactly what was their attitude toward the government, but that in the light of their experience, they thought they could affirm that their people could not have any other feelings except those of perfect loyalty to the federal cause. Rey and all his colleagues forthwith offered their services to General Butler, who had honored them by consulting them on such an important subject. "It goes without saying," continued Mr. Rey, "that I am in accord with the sentiments of my compatriots."

"Good," replied the general, "as a representative of the Federal Government I accept your services." [11]

Fifteen days later, Butler's order came, inviting the population of color to enlist under the banner of liberty. We will state later how the people responded to this call and how General Butler spoke of their zeal, their patriotism, and of their distinguished qualities. Of the committee of four, the two Rey brothers are dead, Edgar Davis and Eugène Rapp survive and live in New Orleans. Let us say further in passing that Mr. St. Albain Sauvinet acted as interpreter in General Butler's office.

---

11. Felix Kuntz records that when General Butler arrived in New Orleans, more than 24,000 Louisiana blacks enlisted in the Union army. Kuntz, *250 Years of Life in New Orleans* (New Orleans: Friends of the Cabildo, Louisiana State Museum, 1968), 73.

Our People and Our History

Mr. Sauvinet was a Creole. There is no doubt that he contributed toward facilitating this interview between General Butler and the associates of Octave Rey.

We should here correct an error that slipped into the history of those times. Some writers claim that the representatives of the free population did not answer General Butler's call and that they took no part in the work of the Reconstruction. These two reports are false. We know that the resolutions adopted by the men of color on April 21, 1861, did not carry a single expression of sentiments obtained through threat, and that consequently they did not involve the consciences of those who had signed them. There is always an exception to the rule. Some of these unfortunate people could have been misled and so believed that it was their duty to remain faithful to the Confederacy, but the number was too few to give rise to any serious reproaches.

The Reys, the Bertonneaus, the Rapps, the Davises, the Larieuxs, the Caillouxs and the Monthieus, the Sent-Manats, the Thibaults, the Detiégés, the Snaërs, the Orions, the Paul Porées, the many others most eminent of our people, not only entered the service but even formed companies, at the invitation given by the general in his proclamation of August 2, 1862.[12]

12. Three companies organized in the fall of 1862, with most of the men arming and uniforming themselves. They were called Native Guards, Louisiana Militia, Confederate States. New Orleans *Picayune*, February 9, 1862. Alice Dunbar Nelson, "People of Color in Louisiana," *Journal of Negro History*, II (January, 1917), 67. When the city fell to the Federals in April, 1862, the guards refused to leave the city; probably they did not want to fight with Confederate forces elsewhere. Charles Vincent, "Negro Leadership in Louisiana, 1862–1870" (M.A. thesis, Louisiana State University, 1968), 7.

On December 25, 1866, Charles W. Gibbons, a 28-year-old black New Orleanian appeared before a committee of the United States House of Representatives. He testified concerning events related to the riot of July 30, 1866, during which he had been arrested twice. Gibbons had been captain of Company K, Third Regiment of Louisiana Native Guards during the Civil War. His testimony included statements concerning the prejudice that existed against black officers, because of which, Gibbons said, he resigned his commission. He stated he had been a free man since infancy.

Blacks were called on to fight for the Confederacy, and they were warned to fight or face exile or execution. He further stated that blacks enlisted often with the intention of deserting as soon as they could, and that some refused to join the Confederate army despite threats to their lives and property.

A Tribute to the Creole People of Color

The greater part of the men whom we have named attended the assembly of April 21, 1861, supposedly in the interests of the Confederacy.[13] Therefore, it is wrong for historians to say that the people of the free black population who wished to die for the cause of slavery, later refused to change their attitude. The stated facts successfully contradict these calumnies, and it is proper that the friends of truth repudiate these lies that tend to discredit men of such honorable and praiseworthy conduct.

The Creoles of high status not only *responded* to the general's call, but they also *took the initiative* and inspired the call when they explained to him the sympathetic attitude of the free population of color. Indeed General Butler hoped to use these Creoles of color as "native guards," but he proceeded more confidently after he learned the sentiments of the entire population. The fact is the free people were at this time the only ones upon whose loyalty the federal government could rely in case of emergency. If it be necessary to furnish further proof of the truth of these statements, one will have to take the trouble to examine the records of Port Hudson.

Let one examine the documents and he will recall the heroic conduct of the First Regiment in this memorable battle. Let him ask who was Captain Cailloux, and the echo of the battlefield will respond triumphantly. Let him ask who was this Arsène whose brains were strewn over the battlefield, and who left large stains of blood on the folds of the flag he carried, from

---

Reports of the Committees of the House of Representatives Made During the Second Session of Thirty-Ninth Congress, 1866–67 (4 vols.; Washington, D.C.: U.S. Government Printing Office, 1867), 124–26, Items 1786 through 1824.

General Butler issued an order, August 22, 1862, recognizing the guards as the legal state militia. He accepted their desertion from the Confederacy with sympathy for the black soldiers. Butler to Edwin M. Stanton, August 14, 1862, *The War of the Rebellion: A Compilation of the Official Records of the Union and Confederate Armies* (Washington, 1800–1901), Ser. 1, Vol. XV, 557.

13. On April 21, 1861, Governor Thomas Overton Moore of Louisiana called an assembly and asked for five thousand volunteers for a year's service, to be received into the Confederate ranks by companies, battalions, or regiments. John D. Winters, *The Civil War in Louisiana* (Baton Rouge: Louisiana State University Press, 1963), 21.

which he was separated only "to render an account to God."[14] That was what he had promised to do. Let the inquirer examine still closer this same flag riddled with seventeen bullet holes and stained with blood. The great General [John Alexander] Logan covered himself with this flag from head to foot in the presence of the regiment, which passed in review, as if to render the highest possible homage to this living symbol of the most sublime devotion.[15]

All these facts should suffice to clarify the doubts of skeptical minds regarding the attitudes and feelings of the leaders of the Creoles of color as they answered General Butler's call in 1862. The Creoles would have had little self-respect if, after Governor Moore's insults, they had held the smallest patriotic regard for the Confederacy.

One might say, perhaps, that the class to which Rey belonged was certainly not the most unfortunate, since it enjoyed special protection. This is true, but this protection, which came sometimes through privileged relatives and sometimes from strangers, had neither the quality nor the necessary influence to make it triumph over the tyranny of race prejudice. It is precisely in the most serious situations that the weakness of this protection was apparent. This fickle, isolated sympathy always yielded under

14. This is possibly a reference to Major Arsène Latour of the War of 1812; he was an engineer, appointed by General Jackson, who worked on the defenses of New Orleans. Edwin A. Davis, *Louisiana: A Narrative History* (Baton Rouge: Claitor's Bookstore, 1965), 179.

15. On May 27, 1863, Port Hudson, located north of Baton Rouge, became the scene of another battle that involved black troops. The First and Third Louisiana Negro regiments raised in New Orleans by General Nathaniel P. Banks were ordered to join the Union troops in an attack on the Confederate defenses. Black Sergeant Planciançois was the Union color bearer. When he fell another man, Corporal Heath, caught up the flag; a third man, a corporal also, took the flag from Heath after he fell and carried it through the rest of the fight. A black lieutenant mounted the Confederate works several times leading his troops, but he finally was mortally wounded. The black regiments of freedmen were led by Captain André Cailloux, a Negro from New Orleans. See Charles Harris Wesley, *Negro Americans in the Civil War: From Slavery to Citizenship* (3 vols.; New York: Publishers Co., Inc., 1967), II, 83, 85, and Chapter II, note 2 of the present volume.

For a detailed description of the action at Port Hudson, see Edward Cunningham, *The Port Hudson Campaign, 1862-1863* (Baton Rouge: Louisiana State University Press, 1963), 82-126.

A Tribute to the Creole People of Color

the pressure of prejudice. Therefore, we can say boldly that Captain Rey must have received only a minimum of protection and absolutely no tolerance. Living between two generations quite different one from the other, he understood his intermediate mission, and he fulfilled his task as best he could. He faced the cannon of war and he participated in the events that the abolition of slavery brought forth. In the midst of all the great, significant happenings of his time, he served his people and his country nobly. It is because of his patriotism, his loyal civil and military services that history must give homage to him. We feel certain that future generations will render justice to his memory.

Chapter XI
The Generation of 1860 ~ The Hero, André Cailloux ~ President Johnson and the Question of the Races ~ Our Political Battles

PATRIOTS AND ADVENTURERS

The generation of 1860 is signally notable for its military service. In 1862 the people furnished two regiments of volunteers to the Union army and several officers to a third regiment. Major Ernest Dumas was among these.[1] The first two regiments were composed of men who were officers and soldiers from our most illustrious free families. These valiant patriots, worthy descendants of their forebears who fought in the wars of 1815 and 1845, burned with the desire to take up arms for the cause of freedom. At the first call for volunteers, they enlisted for three years. They participated in several major battles and impartial history has recorded the quality of their valor.

Even though these same men had been organized militarily by the Confederacy, no occasion was ever given them to display their courage or to test their patriotism. President Lincoln himself had serious doubts as to the loyalty and steadfastness of the black people in the role of soldiers. Time has since answered this question. Soon the entire nation acknowledged the heroism of these men. The bravery and the fearlessness of the Creole troops excited the admiration, not only of the other American people, but of the entire world. The conduct of Captain André Cailloux was adequate proof for the minds of skeptics and it silenced the enemies of the black man.[2]

The eyes of the world were indeed on this American Spartacus.

---

1. François Ernest Dumas served in the Second Regiment and also recruited soldiers, attaching a company of his own slaves to a regiment; he was promoted to the rank of major. He commanded two companies at Pascagoula, Mississippi, during the Civil War. Joseph T. Wilson, *Black Phalanx: A History of the Negro Soldier of the United States in the Wars of 1775–1812, 1861–1865* (New York: Arno Press, 1968), 176.
2. Captain André Cailloux (later Major), a free man before the war,

A Tribute to the Creole People of Color

The hero of ancient Rome displayed no braver heroism than did this officer who ran forward to his death with a smile on his lips and crying, "Let us go forward, O comrades!" Six times he threw himself against the murderous batteries of Port Hudson, and in each assault he repeated his urgent call, "Let us go forward, one more time!" Finally, falling under the mortal blow, he gave his last order to his attending officer, "Bacchus, take charge!" If anyone should say the knightly Bayard did better or more, according to history, he lies.

A point important to the race problem was resolved: André Cailloux certainly proved that the black man is able to fight and die for his country. Our grateful people honored him with an elaborate funeral after the enemy finally released his remains which had lain out on the plains for two months. All those whom Captain Cailloux had glorified by his heroic death came to show their recognition on this solemn occasion. Never before, with one exception, had New Orleans been the theater of such a demonstration. Men, women, and children, all wearing mourning, followed the coffin of this hero to his tomb where his mutilated remains were laid to rest. In all history there was but one André Cailloux! May our compatriots remember him! May they erect a monument or a statue that will save his name from oblivion.

THE CONSTITUTIONAL ASSEMBLY OF 1868

We feel that our work would be singularly incomplete, if we did not add certain observations on the important subject of the Assembly of 1868.

Almost all the Creoles of color who were members of this

---

prided himself in being the blackest individual in New Orleans. He was said to be well educated, with polished manners, as well as bold, athletic, and daring—a splendid horseman and a good boxer. He was killed at Port Hudson. Because of his bravery on the side of the Union, Cailloux became a hero to Union sympathizers in New Orleans. Donald Everett, "Ben Butler and the Louisiana Native Guards, 1861–1862," *Journal of Southern History*, XXIV (May, 1958), 202. See also Mary F. Berry, "Negro Troops in Blue and Gray: The Louisiana Native Guards, 1861–1863," *Louisiana History*, VIII (Spring, 1967), 101.

famous assembly are dead today. History, we think, does not render due justice to the memory of these delegates who were among the first to work toward the peaceful reorganization of our state. There is the danger too that our representatives might become confused with other groups. Hence we feel it is necessary to state for the record the number of our people who attended this convention. It is necessary to examine anew their attitudes and their sentiments during these extraordinary days.

It is important that the Creoles of color be assessed and judged separately because they have always had a will of their own. Let us first state that we were represented in large numbers at the Assembly of 1868, and that if a certain spirit of freedom marked the deliberations of this group, we know for a certainty that the delegates of our race were responsible for this. Despite the heat of the fiery political passions of this time, the conduct of and the decisions made by this sovereign body show no evidence or any sentiment incompatible with reason, justice, and honor. Not the least sign of reprisal, nor the slightest suspicion of hidden rancor, nor a trace of cowardice existed in the Constitution given to the state at that time. On the contrary, by its moderate ordinances, the Constitution exists to the praise of the black delegates to the Assembly. The delegates did their duty as they saw it, voting for universal suffrage, for marriage between races, for civil and political rights of citizens without distinction of color or former status. In other words they expanded the structure of civil privileges for all races instead of placing restraints upon it.[3]

A glance at Article 98 of the Constitution of 1868 will suffice to enlighten any honest and reasonable mind desirous of becom-

---

3. "The Constitutional Convention of April 6, 1864, which abolished slavery, changed much of the status of the Negro population in Louisiana. ... In 1868, with the vote of the Negro and his representation in the House strong, education of the black race seemed assured. By 1869, the Negroes were in the majority vote.... The Southerner did not hate the Negro, but he believed he could not rise sufficiently in the scale of civilization; he believed the franchise was superimposed on the black man by Northern white leadership." Ella Lonn, *Reconstruction in Louisiana After 1868* (New York: Russell and Russell, 1967), 3.

A Tribute to the Creole People of Color

ing informed about the dispositions of the delegates.[4] This article would permit every citizen to enjoy his civil rights from the moment he accepted the system of Reconstruction as stipulated by Congress in 1867. Certainly, it does not owe exclusively to the Creoles of color the fact that liberal measures were adopted, but it is right to make known that they ranged themselves on the side of moderation when there was question of deciding the fate of their adversaries. The future will not be able to reproach them for their actions, for the written proofs they have left in this Constitution of 1868 certify their chivalrous motives and make clear to all that their conduct in the Assembly was magnanimous.

A FORGOTTEN PHASE

The world easily forgets the things of the past, and it is sometimes necessary to recall some of the incidents whose sad recital seems to be too delicate a matter to be often repeated. After the misfortunes that occurred on July 30, 1866, and cost such sacrifices and tears on the part of our people, there resulted something that should never be effaced from our memories.[5] We wish to speak of the great struggle that took place during the administration of President Johnson, as well as of the disap-

---

4. Article 98 of the Constitution of Louisiana, 1868: "Every male person, of the age of twenty-one years or upwards, born or naturalized in the United States, and subject to the jurisdiction thereof, and a resident of this state one year next preceding an election, and the last ten days within the parish in which he offers to vote, shall be deemed an elector, except those disfranchised by this Constitution and persons under interdiction." *Constitution of the State of Louisiana with Amendments Adopted in Convention March 7, 1868* (New Orleans: Republican Office [Printers], 1875), Title VI, General Provisions, 22.

5. Democratic opponents of Negro suffrage vowed to resist Louisiana Governor J. Madison Wells's action in reconvening the 1864 constitutional convention, which they feared would topple their plans to restore a "Confederate democracy." Out of the ensuing political and racial tension came a running street fight in New Orleans on July 30, 1866, that erupted into a vicious battle between whites, blacks, and the police. Almost 200 casualties resulted. Shortly after, by Act of Congress, March 2, 1867, military rule was established in the South and Reconstruction became the order of the day. *Ibid.*, 3–5.

pointments that our people were subjected to at one time or another. We wish to review here openly the virtues of our people who, as they have always done, believed themselves naturally called to take their legitimate and rightful part in the events of their era.

Immediately after the war, there was question of the southern states rejoining the Union. Everyone agreed on the principle of uniting the two sections of the country that four years of war had alienated. Among the leading men of the state there were serious disagreements on the question of principles that should serve as the basis of this reunion. Some favored the idea of *Restoration*; others, the system of *Reconstruction*. These two ideas, although fundamental, were mutually exclusive in practice.

The death of President Lincoln elevated Vice-President Johnson to the first place in the nation. The new chief of state was from Tennessee and history records he was of modest origin, that he felt embarrassed about his beginnings, and that he wished to use his advancement to cover up the status of his ancestry (honorable, no doubt, but too close to the common people). Representatives of the South were perfectly conscious of this situation. They knew the weak side of the President and that this weakness assured them of success in their plans for rehabilitation. They were ready to give their allegiance to the President in exchange for his support in aiding their return to power, with full freedom to direct the situation in their own way and to assess the results of the war. What the conquered states did not wish was to push the results of the war beyond the abolition of slavery. They claimed that their act of placing the federal decree of emancipation in the Constitution should suffice as a measure between the two parties for equity and justice in the solutions of all other questions. This attitude of the heads of the southern states was in accord with that of President Johnson himself. However, despite the sympathy of the President, the southerners were powerless to set aside the plan for the complete liberation of the blacks.

A Tribute to the Creole People of Color

The army was still under the command of Grant, Sherman, and Sheridan, and surely these renowned soldiers, representatives of the martyred President, would never permit the repudiation of the Proclamation of 1863, a measure that had brought under the flag more than 150,000 men whose dedication to the cause of the Union was well known. But the President and his new friends made a political agreement and their actions carried more or less the insinuation of trickery and cunning.

What the southerners wanted was *local self-government*, that is, the administration of their own affairs as in the past, and the reestablishment in each locality of a kind of *feudal law* with no other authority than the will of the master. To achieve this it was necessary that they oppose the absolute liberation of the black man, as well as universal suffrage. They thought that in order to insure the realization of their ends, it was necessary to stop the increase in the number of citizens whose ideals were contrary to theirs. To gain public support, they began by complaining that the North intended to humiliate them by subjecting them to the authority and the domination of their former slaves.

This was only a pretext. The southerners wished to have power. Thy wished still more to avenge themselves on the man of color, as they admitted later. The man of color had served under the Union flag to combat the Confederacy, and that in their eyes was a crime. Even today the poor black man suffers for having subscribed to the cause of freedom.

The leaders in the North did not believe the South was sufficiently reconciled to the new regime to act in good faith or to be guided in its decisions by a spirit of humanity. They held the reins of power, and they were under a moral obligation to the man of color freshly returned from the field of battle, where he had displayed his valor in defense of his country. It would have been an act of insanity on their part to lose the political advantage that was inherent in universal suffrage. For this reason the leaders of the Republican party supported the regenerating idea of Reconstruction. They resolved, therefore, to make some changes in the federal Constitution and to suppress the conspiracies that could stop or interfere with the execution of their plans.

President Johnson, who had his own small ambitions in the matter, took sides with the conquered states. It was a known fact that he used all his official and personal power to place in their hands the control of the state governments of the South, with no regard for fairness or respect for the wishes of Congress, which he did not even consult. It is evident that the President's scheme was to place at the good pleasure of these states the civil and political destinies of the man of color. This was what they called *Restoration*—a method of rewarding the guilty and punishing the innocent.

This attitude of the President complicated the situation. We must respect his convictions, but we cannot approve them. It was necessary to fight them, not because of him, but because of the ill effects that would follow. These effects would prevent the man of color from becoming a citizen, and God knows if the Union itself would then have survived. Because the President persisted in the ill use of his supreme power, Congress resolved to impeach him. The result of this procedure was to reduce him to powerlessness and to strip him of prestige.

The battle between him and those giants of the Reconstruction was dedicated as much to the interests of the blacks as to the salvation of the country. Events have proved this, because for a short while after the victory of the northerners, there was more recognition given the man of color in the Black Code [*Code Noir* promulgated in 1724 by Bienville].

It is evident that in such a situation the Creole population could not remain inactive or indifferent and leave it to others to undergo the labor and the suffering. There were two factions among them: one, under the direction of the attorney Thomas J. Durant,[6] organized the Radical Republican Club in 1865 in

---

6. Thomas J. Durant, who organized the Radical Republican Club in 1865, was a lawyer and a prewar Douglas Democrat faction leader. He worked with Dr. Charles Roudanez and his son Jean Baptiste, Arnold Ber-

A Tribute to the Creole People of Color

the *Salle d'Economie*; the other faction was under the leadership of the Reverend Dostie, an intrepid man who never recoiled in the face of any danger and never stopped before any obstacle.[7] The plan of the Radical Club on the advice of Mr. Durant was to entrust itself entirely to the good will of Congress in Washington. Following this decision the members of this club refrained from participating in the Convention of July 30, 1866.

Dostie, on the contrary, had conceived the idea of trying a daring step that would precipitate matters. Unfortunately for him and his followers, they met too many insurmountable obstacles: their efforts and sacrifices were futile. They have left us only a remembrance of sorrow and regret. This tactical error caused the death of several honest Creoles of color, who lost their lives without having the honor of uttering the first word of their aspirations. Nevertheless, the Reconstruction triumphed. The federal Constitution was amended, and from 1865 to 1870, all citizens without exception were admitted to the privilege of voting. This was the decisive result that had been the hope of Durant's Radical Club, and his expectation had not been in vain.[8]

THE LEADERS OF THE PARTY   Leaders of the parties of this period included Dr. Louis Roudanez, J. B. Roudanez, Arnold Bertonneau, Oscar J. Dunn, Aristide Mary, Thomy Lafon, Victor Macarty, Laurent Auguste, Antoine Dubuclet, J. P. Lanna, Paul Trévigne, and Formidor Desmazilière. There were still others

---

tonneau, Oscar Dunn, Aristide Mary, Thomy Lafon, Victor Macarty, Antoine Dubuclet, and other black leaders. Donald Everett, "Demands of the New Orleans Free Colored Population for Political Equality, 1852–1865," *Louisiana Historical Quarterly*, XXXVIII (April, 1955), 60–61.

7. A. P. Dostie was a dentist; he was a pronounced Unionist and strong abolitionist. Dostie died of a gunshot wound received in the July 30, 1866, riot in New Orleans. John Rose Ficklen, *History of Reconstruction in Louisiana Through 1868* (Baltimore: The Johns Hopkins University Press, 1910), 167.

8. In 1865 Negroes voted for the first time in Louisiana and the Creoles of color actively entered the political field. Roland Wingfield, "The Creoles of Color: A Study of a New Orleans Subculture" (M.A. thesis, Louisiana State University, 1961), 185.

but we cannot recall their names. These are men who fought in the name of justice. These valiant Creoles were the first people in Louisiana to offer themselves as champions of a movement whose purpose was the establishment in the state of the principle of universal suffrage, a measure destined to become part of the amendments to the Constitution. These men were animated by the purest patriotism and their sincerity equaled their righteousness. They came from all ranks of society. But their common goal united them as one, despite contrasts in their occupations and financial status. From childhood they had learned the meaning of respectability, and when the time came to act, they gave proof of all the qualities that can inspire love and confidence.

Their situation placed them above all temptations, and their proud natures sheltered them from all kinds of seductions. There can be only one way of directing such worthy men and that is to appeal to their honor and sense of duty, to show them the right road, and to present cooly the arguments of truth and justice. These generous servants of the common cause no doubt lacked experience, but they were provided with enlightened councilors whose wise advice kept them within permissible limits. They gave liberally of their money, their concern, and their efforts to bring about the triumph of the *principles* that they believed to be the best. They asked only their place at the banquet of life, although they were, as Gilbert said, "unhappy revelers." In the light of these facts, it would be unjust to hold them responsible for the extravagances that have since marred the holy cause of freedom and political equality.

These men held the principles of justice too dear to promote or to participate in exploitation and corruption. It is true they were approached in the hope they would be the tools of ignominious fraud and trickery, but they rebelled at the mere thought of this sort of action. There were of course a few exceptions to the rule, but these are not worthy of mention.

The patriots founded first of all the weekly newspaper *L'Union* to serve as their voice. Paul Trévigne became its man-

A Tribute to the Creole People of Color

aging editor. Among the contributors was Nelson Fouché, a brilliant but exceedingly modest man, whose genius was respected by all races. He has left us a small volume entitled *Nouveau Recueil* [*A New Harvest*]. The book reveals the ambitions and hopes he had for progress in our society. Fouché busied himself mostly with painting, surveying, and the arts.

Affairs moved along rather rapidly. However, the founders of *L'Union* felt this paper lacked impact; therefore, in its stead they founded *La Tribune de la Nouvelle-Orléans*. It was a daily newspaper owned by the celebrated Dr. Roudanez, with Mr. Dalloz as editor, and Paul Trévigne, Sr., as associate editor. Mr. Dalloz came from Belgium. A learned man and a friend of the oppressed, he put all his ardor and talents into the service of the cause he embraced. The principles of Dr. Roudanez and his associates were fully discussed and promoted in the columns of *La Tribune*. Because of the high character of these men, their righteous intentions, their great knowledge, and their vast experience, and even more because of their superb spirit of independence, these leaders acquired a prestige that made them as powerful in Washington as in New Orleans.[9] The Creole population thus was united, for the people trusted the honesty

9. Dr. Louis Charles Roudanez (1823–90) was born in St. James Parish; he died in New Orleans. He studied medicine in New Orleans and Europe. He founded *La Tribune*, which was the first Negro daily newspaper in the United States. Roudanez was convinced that the Carpetbaggers were using Negroes as tools to build their own power, and that they had no real interest in the black race itself. Because *La Tribune* did not support the candidates chosen by the 1868 Republican convention, François Ernest Dumas (see note 1 above) lost the race for lieutenant governor. Shortly afterward, Roudanez retired from all activities except his medical practice. When the Unification movement failed in 1873, he again felt the sting of unpopularity. Finnian P. Leavens, "*L'Union* and the New Orleans *Tribune* and Louisiana Reconstruction" (M.A. thesis, Louisiana State University, 1966), 1–20.

According to Edward Larocque Tinker, "Mr. Dalloz" was Jean Charles (Houzheau), a Belgian, born in Mons in 1820. He was a member of the Royal Academy of Science of Belgium and was exiled because of his Republican activities. Houzeau came to America in 1857 and to New Orleans in 1864. He joined the abolitionists and wrote under a pen name "Cham," or "C. J. Dalloz." He edited *L'Union*. It was through his sympathies with Roudanez' cause that he accepted the editorship of *La Tribune*. He is said to have had underground influence in Reconstruction politics. Tinker, *Creole City: Its Past and Its People* (New York: Longmans, Green, 1953), 107–108.

and patriotism of these men, who had so generously taken upon themselves responsibility for their people's political salvation.

THE ADVENTURERS The adventurers of this era were quick to make themselves known. Their presence in our meetings was soon noticed. With their eyes fixed on power, they gathered together in a common effort to assure the success of their ambitious plots. Having observed that the men of *La Tribune* were the sworn enemies of corruption and oppression, they leagued themselves against them and vowed a fight to the death. Their first objective was the disorganization of the central committee. All their resources and energies were commandeered to this end.

One can readily understand why these ambitious people would not associate themselves with men who fought against the whole idea of systematic subjugation and who refused to consent to their own debasement. They were convinced they would achieve no victory unless the true friends of the people withdrew. Therefore they resolved to interest the "new citizens [freedmen]" in their schemes. These latter were incapable of making a correct estimation of people and events, and thus they let themselves be duped and seduced by a thousand loose promises.

Graft, corruption, lies, violence, and even class hatred—all were used to destroy the closely united patriots of *La Tribune*. Dr. Roudanez and his associates asked only for justice and equality for all before the law. In no way did they intend to begin a reign of license or disorder. But demagoguery misrepresented everything. For our friends at *La Tribune*, it was a case of shielding people from proscription and avoiding the granting of privileges to anyone because of race or color.

Some of these people were exiles from France, true friends of liberty who found an opportunity to make themselves useful by promoting better conditions for their fellow men in this country that the illustrious Lafayette had stained with his blood.

A Tribute to the Creole People of Color

They also wished to encourage among our people respect for the rights of all citizens and to discourage an excess of corrupting ambition and ignorance. These leaders were too honorable, too sincere in their high sense of duty to have recourse to strategems of baseness or deceit. They spoke the truth to everyone and accepted delay whenever necessary in the presence of complications that were dangerous and difficult to analyze. If this policy of patience and restraint had been followed throughout, success, though slower in coming, would have become a reality. But others wished to hurry events, and the terrible reaction proved fatal to all of us. The noble leaders of our people operating *La Tribune* ceased to resist out of pure disgust. Let us hasten to add, however, that the reign of knaves and adventurers was of short duration. When faced with the supreme crisis, all fell into the same abyss of defeat and humiliating failure. The embezzlement and treachery attributed to them is a matter of history, although all the accusations against them have not been proved.

No longer able to meet publication expenses and experiencing only disappointments and betrayal, *La Tribune* ceased operation. The champions of our liberty had to be content with murmuring privately against the injustice of the oppressor and the secret schemes of the corrupting forces that ruled the councils of the [Republican] party. Although the ranks of our friends were weakened, they were not completely wiped out. The deserters were only pygmies. The giants were still capable of making themselves feared when the need arose and when they wished to bother to enter the lists. Unfortunately, they lost the new generation, which let itself be absorbed by the influences of the times. Consequently, little by little, death did its work and our noble leaders of 1860 finally disappeared. At the time of the unexpected transition after the crisis of 1877, only a handful of them were left.

And that is why they made a supreme effort against the first signs of the reactionary movement whose policy prevails even to this day with the most alarming effects. When Governor

Nicholls took office, one of his first acts was to segregate the school children according to their color.[10] This was the first blow of the knife under the agreement between President Hayes and the Democratic leaders of the state who had all promised to help him into office. Our patriots, who were faithful to their principles of equality, considered the new policy dishonorable. They went to the Public School Office to protest against this arbitrary rule. They visited the governor, who was supposedly sympathetic, and made the same complaints to him. Unfortunately, their pleas met with no success. The government, obeying the spirit of the Democratic party, was immovable. The decision stood to construct separate school facilities to receive children of each race where they would be instructed separately.

For a while the majority of the black people, seduced perhaps by appearances, seemed to prefer segregation of their community, notwithstanding the loss of prestige and various advantages brought by this policy of isolation. This difference of opinion on the vital question was contrary to the welfare of our children, and it made impossible any understanding between the men at *La Tribune* and the disciples of the new school. The old defenders of our rights attended the meetings of the general Constitutional Convention held under the chairmanship of Lieutenant Governor Louis A. Wiltz in 1879.[11] Several black delegates (of American birth) registered as accredited members. It was at this convention that an ordinance was adopted to

---

10. Francis Redding Tillou Nicholls (1834–1912) was born in Donaldsonville, Louisiana, and died at Thibodaux, Louisiana. He was a West Point graduate and studied law at Louisiana State University. In 1877 he was elected the first governor of his native state after the Reconstruction period; he served a second term in 1888. In 1892 he became chief justice of the state supreme court. *Dictionary of American Biography*, s.v. Nicholls, Francis Redding Tillou.

11. Louis Alfred Wiltz (1843–81), a Democrat, was a member of the New Orleans Common Council. He was elected mayor of New Orleans in 1872. He was a successful candidate for speaker of the legislature in 1875, supported by the Democrats against the Radical Republican group and Governor Kellogg. He was elected lieutenant governor of Louisiana in 1876 on the ticket with Governor Nicholls. In 1879 he was president of the state constitutional convention and in the same year was elected governor of Louisiana. He died during his term of office.

A Tribute to the Creole People of Color

establish Southern University for the higher education of black children in the state.[12]

The black delegates accepted this ordinance that, on principle alone, was a contradiction of what had previously been done to obliterate in this state all discrimination by race before the law. It was this legislation that Mr. Mary had called the "Black League in the Constitution." The black people whose weakness led them to sanction the principle of segregation of the races had already figured in the Assembly of 1868; logically, they should not have attended it if they were not able to stand up for their rights. Certainly, giving the appearance of consenting to their own debasement was not a role that suited the representatives of the oppressed. But the mentality of a large number of these political persons was such that they were never able to understand the serious aspect of life—that is, the true meaning of duty. After these events, which grieved our former champions, people no longer spoke of them as an active and leading power in our political quarrels. This was the end. The black man had accepted legal subordination—that is, the idea of being treated conventionally and not constitutionally.

The vote of these representatives helped to create a system they knew would deprive the black children of the advantages of education available to other children of our state. These men

---

12. The first Louisiana public schools (1841) did not admit blacks; until after the Civil War private instruction was the main source of education for the few Negroes who could afford it. The founding of the Couvent school in 1848 presaged a gradual growth of private schools in the later nineteenth century. The first public schools in New Orleans that admitted blacks were organized by the Federal army in 1861–1865. John H. Rohrer and Munro S. Edmondson, *The Eighth Generation: Cultures and Personalities of New Orleans Negroes* (New York: Harper, 1960), 34.

In 1900 there were 2,637,774 blacks ten years of age and older in the southern states. Charles W. Dabney, *Universal Education in the South* (2 vols.; Chapel Hill: University of North Carolina Press, 1936), II, 408–12. See also C. Vann Woodward, *Origins of the New South, 1877–1913* (Baton Rouge: Louisiana State University Press, 1951), 365–98, 400.

Only in the late twentieth century did blacks begin to participate normally in the education system. In 1950 blacks comprised 32 percent of the total New Orleans population, but black children amounted to 98 percent of the children in public schools. Rohrer and Edmondson, *The Eighth Generation*, 34.

Our People and Our History

knew that this line of demarcation, once established, chiefly by their consent, would serve as the basis and the pretext for other measures contrary to the interests and rights of our citizens. They knew that this action on their part was a move of regression, that they were sacrificing all the progress that the past had consecrated and that they themselves had worked to obtain.

OF UNIFICATION We must speak of the Unification movement, a significant episode in the political career of our leaders, one often misjudged for lack of understanding.[13] The reader will undoubtedly recall the reply that Benjamin Constant made to Napoleon Bonaparte when the latter asked the author of the "Additional Act of 1815" if he were a Bonapartist or a Bourbonist. "I am a patriot," cooly responded this citizen to the emperor.[14] Above all else our great patriots were men of principle. When the noble citizens who had conceived the plan of unification invited these men to join them, they did so without the least hesitation. Guided by a sense of duty, they were ready to follow any light that would lead them along the way to well-being.

The plan of unification contained every assurance and guarantee for the enjoyment of liberty and justice. In the minds of our leaders, a happy and prosperous future lay ahead. Like Benjamin Constant, the name counted for nothing—only the resultant work was important.

We read that Formidor Desmazilière, one day in discussing the movement, observed to some of his friends that he did not ask if such and such a person were a Republican, a Democrat, or a liberal, because his one desire was to be considered just another man in his own country, in the country that his father had defended against foreign invasion. "Since," he added, "these

---

13. For a discussion of the Unification movement, see T. Harry Williams, "The Louisiana Unification Movement of 1873," *Journal of Southern History*, XI (August, 1945), 349–69.

14. Benjamin Constant (1767–1830) was a French author and political leader with liberal views. His best-known literary effort is his novel *Adolphe* (1816).

A Tribute to the Creole People of Color

gentlemen recognize our rights; since they promise us even half of the benefits that are by natural right due those associated in a common enterprise; since, in a word, finally they guarantee us liberty, equality, and fraternity; we have nothing more to ask. Our duty is but to cooperate with those who assure us peace, order, and progress, whatever be their title or their ancestors."

The time has come to prove the wisdom of this reasoning. The movement failed, but we have retained the memory of it. If it did not succeed, it was because it was premature. The people were not prepared to renounce their way of thinking: we could not hope to see them ratify a policy destined to reverse long-established customs.

Chapter XII
Politics and the Sense of Duty ⁓
Mr. Aristide Mary and the Citizens'
Committee ⁓ Our Last Entrenchments ⁓
Defections and Failings ⁓ Our Last Thank You

POLITICS AND THE SENSE OF DUTY

The men of *La Tribune* who in 1872 proposed the candidacy of Aristide Mary for governor of the state were inspired by a sense of political duty. We say "the men of *La Tribune*," because we want to speak of those who had never compromised, of those who remained faithful to the principles of justice and of equality. The idea was not to impose Aristide Mary upon the Republican masses because he was a man of color: they wanted solely to oppose a moral resistance against the deadly doctrine of exclusion. In other words I will say that the supporters of Aristide Mary laid claim to the *right of aspiring* to the position of governor, but they did not actually covet the post itself.

Mary had sufficient good sense and enough patriotism and experience to appreciate the difficulties of the situation. He knew well that in the Convention of 1872 money had established the laws and that slaves who sold their votes could only obey, even against principles. He was prepared for defeat, but his name on the ballot was like defiance thrown into the face of prejudice. Mary knew that the majority at this convention was composed of speculators and that even among his own people these traits could be found. But he did not complain. He represented solely the idea of political duty, and he considered himself most fortunate to have maintained enough influence to command respect for his aspirations, convictions, and principles.

The people have the right to be very proud of Aristide Mary and of all those who, like him, never recoiled when faced with truth. Their virtures have done honor to us and their sacrifices have elevated us. For this, we owe them much gratitude.

Mary lived long enough to suggest the formation of a Citi-

A Tribute to the Creole People of Color

zens' Committee which was composed of eighteen members: this was the last political act he performed. We see there the proof that, despite his seventy years, his sense of duty was still strong and he respected its dictates, as he said, "Cost what it may!"

MR. ARISTIDE MARY AND THE CITIZENS' COMMITTEE

It was in 1890 that the Citizens' Committee was formed, when a return to exaggerated fanaticism about caste or segregation once again alarmed the black people. This fanaticism was not confined merely to chance meetings. We were face to face with a government determined to develop and establish a system by which a portion of the people would have to submit to the rest.

It was necessary to resist this state of affairs, even with no hope of success in sight. Mary's idea was to give a dignified appearance to the resistance, which had to be implemented by lengthy judicial procedures. The committee was composed of: Arthur Estèves, president; C. Antoine, vice-president; Firmin Christophe, secretary; G. G. Johnson, undersecretary; Paul Bonseigneur, treasurer; Laurent Auguste, R. L. Desdunes, Alcée Labat, Pierre Chevalier, N. E. Mansion, A. B. Kennedy, R. B. Baqué, A. J. Guirenovich, L. A. Martinet [founder of the *Daily Crusader*], L. J. Joubert, M. J. Piron, Eugène Luscy, E. A. Williams. The group organized itself in New Orleans, September 5, 1891. This committee, in an address published in the columns of the *Crusader*, made itself publicly known, explained its purpose and determination, and asked the public for donations to help it in its patriotic enterprise. In a short time, it had collected a considerable sum. It then was able to proceed without difficulty with its double mission involving a legal battle and the dissemination of propaganda. From the outset the organization received strong and valuable support from various parts of the country. Among the eminent men who responded to our call, we may cite with pride the Honorable Albion W. Tourgée and John

M. Harlan—one, an outspoken champion of black people; the other, one of the nine judges of the United States Supreme Court. The people should never forget these noble men, particularly Tourgée. He shed his blood on the battlefield on the side of the Union. After the war he lived among the oppressed, defending their cause at peril of his life, as he describes the situation in his work *The Fool's Errand*.[1]

For more than thirty years, he fought solely for the cause of the education of the underprivileged, for their development and their advancement toward a better future under the protection of American institutions. He was one of the first to offer his services to the Citizens' Committee, which showed its appreciation by retaining him as its principal legal adviser. Mr. Walker and Mr. Martinet were his associates. The people soon recognized the value of this association.

But the legal side was not the only one that received Tourgée's attention. As a defender of the weak, he filled the columns of the *Inter-Ocean* [Chicago newspaper] with his relentlessly logical articles that testified to our daily living conditions. We may say of Judge Harlan that he was always firm and just in each of the decisions of the high court, of which he was a most capable member for thirty-three years. He always voted against any measure that tended to degrade a citizen or scorn the Constitution.

The Citizens' Committee had as its mission to protest the adoption and enforcement of the statutes that established the

---

1. Albion Winegar Tourgée (1838–1905) was an American jurist and author; he was born in Williamsfield, Ohio, and died in Bordeaux, France, where he was consul. From 1868 to 1874 he was judge of the Superior Court of North Carolina; during his term of office, he was a vigorous foe of the Ku Klux Klan. Sworn statements by many Klan members were later used by Tourgée in works of fiction dealing with Reconstruction in the South; *A Fool's Errand* (1879) was the best known of these books. *Encyclopedia Americana*, International ed., s.v., Tourgée, Albion Winegar.

John Marshall Harlan (1833–1911) was an American jurist; he was born in Boyle County, Kentucky, and died in Washington, D.C. He was attorney general of Kentucky from 1863 to 1867. A Republican, he was appointed a member of Grant's commission to investigate the fraudulent 1876 election in Louisiana. In that same year he was appointed associate justice of the United States Supreme Court and served in this post until his death. *Encyclopedia Americana*, International ed., s.v. Harlan, John Marshall.

A Tribute to the Creole People of Color

unjust and humiliating discrimination against the black race in Louisiana. But it was particularly concerned with Act 111 of 1890. This act was the result of a policy begun in 1877. It was foreseen that in trains there would be separate accommodations for whites and blacks; however, as the act contained clauses that affected the railroads' providing traffic between states, the committee had no difficulty in obtaining an annulment of it. We must say that prior to the passage of this law, a delegation of black citizens had visited the capital of the state to present the grievances of our people to the General Assembly.

Their protests met with no success. We had counted on the possible support of certain generous men such as those who lived in 1879 and on the supposed patriotism of some black legislators. But all these hopes failed. The law, in a modified form, was adopted despite the presence of these black representatives who claimed great influence, they said, because they had close connections with the Louisiana Lottery Company, at that time considered all powerful. It is often said that, far from doing us good, their relations with this corporation had done much to turn people against blacks in general. Surely their position was embarrassing, and it is doubtful that they were sufficiently independent to be seriously concerned with the wishes and rights of a people under fire.

In any case the delegation of 1890 achieved no satisfaction from anyone. We therefore resolved to begin the legal battle and we chose Mr. Daniel Desdunes [a son of Rodolphe Desdunes] to take the first steps against Act 111. In conformity with the plans of the committee, Mr. Desdunes was arrested by one of the members of the secret police for having obtained passage in a train reserved by law exclusively for whites. He was put on trial, which was of short duration, as the court decided that the law was unconstitutional, in that it was not compatible with the federal Constitution—as the law supported prejudice concerning the rights of transportation between states. Mr. Desdunes was therefore acquitted.

The second law forbade the mixing of races in the conveyances traveling from one place to another within a state. To attack this second ruling the Committee engaged Mr. Homère Plessy as its representative. When his action in the criminal court of the state failed, the committee made an appeal as a last resort.[2] After the case had rested for several months, the federal Supreme Court, with Justice Harlan dissenting, rejected this appeal and the committee was then obliged to submit to the inevitable; that is, they had to pay a fine of twenty-five dollars. Thus terminated the second legal action instituted in the name of the people against the validity of Act 111 and others. Our defeat sanctioned the odious principle of the *segregation of races.*

We should have said that the Plessy case had been pleaded in the first instance before Judge Ferguson with Mr. Lionel Adams as attorney for the prosecution, and Mr. James Walker as representative of the committee. The state's lawyer had proceeded under the theory of *contact-répugnant* and sustained the constitutionality of a law based on such a theory. He related to the court how certain passengers had been greatly inconvenienced by the odors resulting from too much close contact with certain persons of color and this argument sufficed to establish the legality of the law. Mr. Walker spoke at length for the defense. He said that he could not conceive how the state could condemn a group of its citizens in order to appease the repugnance of others, that Blackstone should be placed above dictionaries when the definition of offenses was given, and that this master of jurisprudence did not leave any text on which one might base the justification for distinctions made between the races. But the magnificent plea for the defense made by Mr. Walker

2. The *Comité des Citoyens* especially concentrated on and was successful in defeating through judicial action Act III of the Louisiana legislature of 1870, known as the "Jim Crow Law." It was this group that brought the *Plessy* v. *Ferguson* case to the courts. Otto H. Olsen (ed.), *The Thin Disguise: Turning Point in Negro History, Plessy v. Ferguson, A Documentary Presentation, 1864–1896* (New York: Humanities Press, 1967), 69.

Two years later the state constitutional convention adopted the "grandfather clause," that disfranchised almost 90 percent of the state's black population of voting age. See Roland Wingfield, "The Creoles of Color: A Study of a New Orleans Subculture" (M.A. thesis, Louisiana State University, 1961), 189.

A Tribute to the Creole People of Color

could not change anything that had been resolved. Henceforth nothing else could be expected other than continuation of this policy by which people were divided into upper and lower class according to their color and origin.

The committee did not even attempt to contest the law which forbade marriage between the races. It attacked, however, the moral issues of the law and at a suitable time and place it presented to the General Assembly of the state a petition, respectful, but full of reasonable objections. Despite the predominant hostility, it received high expressions of sympathy from certain members of the legislative body. Among the number of these friends of justice we will list the Senators Tissot and Caffery, both of whom are dead today.[3] Their labor as defenders of morals and liberty will never be forgotten. There were yet others but they took no direct part in the battle as did the two gentlemen we have just named.

Senator Caffery was the president of the judiciary committee in charge of the draft bill. Judge Tissot himself held the floor a long time in opposition to this arbitrary measure. Archbishop Janssens took an active part in the question under debate.[4] In one letter that the eminent prelate had the kindness to send to

---

3. A. L. Tissot was a native New Orleans lawyer. He was a Democrat, a member of the Louisiana Senate, once district judge of Orleans. *Biennial Report of the State of Louisiana, General Assembly, 1892–1893* (Baton Rouge: Baton Rouge *Advocate*, Official Journal of the State of Louisiana, 1894), 101. And see *Louisiana Historical Quarterly*, XXVII (January, 1944), 984.

Donelson Caffery (1835–1906) was born near Franklin, Louisiana. He was a lawyer and sugar planter. A Democrat, in 1892 he was elected to the Louisiana Senate and was appointed to the United States Senate in the same year to fill out the unexpired term of Randall L. Gibson who had died in office. He was one of the Louisiana antilottery leaders who succeeded in getting a state law passed that put the lottery out of business. Clayton Rand, *Stars in Their Eyes: Dreamers and Builders in Louisiana* (Gulfport, Miss.: Dixie Press, 1953), 165.

4. Archbishop Francis Xavier Janssens (1843–97) was born in Tilbury, Holland. He was educated at the Grand Seminary of Bois le Duc and ordained at the American Seminary, Louvain, 1867. He served as a pastor in Richmond, Virginia, in 1881. He was consecrated bishop of Natchez and later was made archbishop of New Orleans. *The New Catholic Encyclopedia* (New York: McGraw-Hill Publ. Co., 1967), X, s.v. New Orleans Archdiocese.

Senator Caffery, he termed the new law a violation of the liberty of conscience. All these measures had been taken at the solicitation of the Citizens' Committee. The agitation caused by this committee and the *Crusader* produced its fruits: the bill drafted against the sacrament of marriage and individual liberty was not even deliberated. Nevertheless, this hateful measure inspired by prejudice was soon to reappear.

In 1894 debate on the question was resumed and in 1896, the law was finally adopted in full force. It was called the Gauthreaux Law.[5] Let us say that Mr. Gauthreaux until then had not feared to uphold the side of justice. In 1894 there was neither intervention nor intercession. The people remained abandoned to their miseries, to such an extent that they could look upon Christian charity as a novel paradox.

The committee had lost its defenders: the archbishop remained inactive; Senator Tissot was dead; Senator Caffery had been elevated to the United States Senate. The cooperation of these three men had been the keystone of our hopes. When they left us, we were left without support, without consolation. Without these leaders other supporters naturally changed their attitudes. The most timid among these fickle people conceded through fear of threats. The others obeyed because of different motives, but all without exception returned to their old allegiances.

Despite these disappointments the committee did not become discouraged. It still had the *Crusader* at its sevice, a daily paper founded by the Honorable Louis A. Martinet. This paper was most influential. It was published under the auspices of an office of directors, but under the editorship and immediate control of Mr. Martinet. He was conscientious, energetic, and

---

5. Charles Gauthreaux was a native New Orleans lawyer; in 1893 he was thirty-one years old. See *Biennial Report of the State of Louisiana . . . 1892–1893*, 101. By Act 54, Section 1 constitutes an amendment and reenactment of Article 94 of the Revised Civil Code of Louisiana of 1870, prohibiting marriage between white persons and persons of color. See *Acts Passed by the General Assembly of the State of Louisiana at the Regular Session* (Baton Rouge: Baton Rouge *Advocate*, Official Journal of the State of Louisiana, 1894), 63.

A Tribute to the Creole People of Color

talented, and he commanded respect through his courage and his fidelity to Republican principles.

Uncompromising in his ideas, invincible in his perseverance, precise and yet varied in his style, he reflected in the columns of his newspaper the hopes of his people in all their strength and integrity. But this paper, however useful and independent it showed itself in expressing its views and in fulfilling commitments, however powerful it seemed to be in the community, was doomed like its predecessors, doomed to fail through lack of support.

We can attribute this failure only to discouragement on the part of some and to the poverty of others. Those who had the means and who would have been able to support the paper were frightened at the increasingly difficult circumstances. Seeing that the friends of justice were either dead or indifferent, they believed that the continuation of the *Crusader* would not only be fruitless but decidedly dangerous. Seeing too that the tyranny of their oppressors was limitless, that they were using all their genius to multiply degrading laws against blacks, our people believed it was better to suffer in silence than to attract attention to their misfortune and weakness. We do not share this reasoning. We think that it is more noble and dignified to fight, no matter what, than to show a passive attitude of resignation.

Absolute submission augments the oppressor's power and creates doubt about the feelings of the oppressed. Mr. Arthur Estèves, president of the committee, was indeed a patriot, active and devoted. He fulfilled his duty to the end. He was a man on whom the people could count in every kind of venture. Like Mr. Bonseigneur, he was entirely dedicated to the cause. He rendered great service for which our people should show everlasting gratitude.

Mr. Estèves, before joining the *Comité des Citoyens* [Citizens' Committee], had already acquired a certain reputation as president of the directors of the [Couvent] school for indigent orphans. He was the man whom the people had chosen in 1884 to lift this institute from ruin. By his honesty, his labors and his generosity, he not only put the school back on its feet, but he contributed materially to augmenting its resources. A man who had obtained such good results easily gains the confidence of others. At the first meeting of the committee, he was unanimously elected chairman, which position he occupied with honor to the end. The people may rejoice in having had such defenders for their cause—men like Bonseigneur, Martinet, and Estèves. Not the least suspicion sullied the purity of their actions during the four years in which they conducted the battles of the committee. Estèves was of a Louisiana family, but was Haitian by birth. He died in New Orleans in 1906 at the age of seventy-one. At the time of his death, he was working as a sailmaker.

OUR LAST THANK YOU

As for Mr. Bonseigneur, he could really be called *the man* of 1890! After the organization of the Citizens' Committee, it was necessary to move with extreme caution. The committee was seeking justice; therefore it was necessary to be prepared to conform to the formalities imposed. From the moment that Mr. Bonseigneur had said to the members of the committee, "I am with you," he placed himself entirely at their disposal. He attended every meeting and supported the patriotic enthusiasm of the members. He appeared everywhere that his presence, prudence, or advice were needed for the common good. In fact he was, so to speak, the mainspring of the committee's actions, an indispensable influence for the progress and the development of its plans and activities.

Thanks to him, each move of the committee was a success. Not one of its plans went awry. The courts, it is true, rejected our demands, but thanks to the good and loyal labors of Mr. Bonseigneur, our people had the satisfaction of pushing the American government to the wall by acting through the ministry of one of its constituent branches. A worthy son of a veteran of 1814–1815, this valiant citizen resisted the unprecedented usurpation inspired by hatred and prejudice to the best of his ability. Future generations will remember him.

Index

Abeilard, Joseph, 71, 72
Abeilard, Jules, 72
Adams, Lionel, 144
Afro-French poems, 5n
Aldiger Committee, 75
Antoine, C., 141
Assembly of April 21, 1861, pp. 120, 121
Assembly of 1868, p. 137
Athénée Louisianais, 65
August, Laurent, 131, 141
"Au Printemps" (poem), 46

Bacchus, Noel, 26, 77, 107
Banks, Nathaniel P., 122n
Barrès, Basile, 86, 87
Baton Rouge, La., xi, 122n
Beaumont, Joseph, 61, 62, 63, 64
Béranger, Pierre Jean, 10n, 64n
Berchmans Home, 92
Bertonneau, Arnold, 131
Black, Code. *See* Code Noir
Boisdoré, François, 79, 80
Boise, Jean, 42, 46
Boise, Louis, 46
Bonseigneur, Paul, 141, 147, 148
Booth, John Wilkes, 9
Bowers, [?], 43
Brown, John, of Kansas, 111
Brulé, Emilien, 21
Butler, John, 22, 118–22

Caffery, Donelson, 145, 146
Cailloux, Andre Capt., 121, 122n, 124–25
Campaign of 1814–15, pp. 5, 81
Canonge, Louis Placide, 109
Castra, Hippolyte, 3, 4, 5n, 7, 8

Catholic Church, 97, 98, 105, 107n, 109
Catholic institute for indigent orphans, (Bernard Couvent institute), 14, 16, 21, 22, 23n, 65, 68, 101n, 102n, 104, 106n, 107n, 108, 114, 118, 147
Cazenave, Pierre, 80
Chalmette, Battle of, 4, 81
"Chant d'amour" (poem), 12, 37
"Chantes la noce d'un ami" (poem), 50
Charbonnet, Charles, 107
Chaumette, Alexandre, 76, 77n
Chevalier, Pierre, 141
Christophe, Firmin, 141
Citizens' Committee, (Comite des Citoyens), xv, 95, 140–42, 144, 146–48
Civil War, xiii, 14n, 23n, 56n, 61, 71, 79n, 80, 83, 91, 106n, 107, 114, 120n, 124n, 137n
Claiborne, William C. C., 3n, 81n
Code Noir, x, xix, 4, 130
Confederacy, 23, 120n, 121n, 122, 124, 129
Confederate army, 14n, 22, 122
Constitution of the United States, 128, 130, 131, 132, 142, 143
Constitutional Assembly of 1868, pp. 125, 126
Convent of the holy family, 92
Courrier français, 109n
Couvent, Gabriel Bernard, 101n, 103n
Couvent, Justine Fervin, 17, 21, 22, 23, 97, 99, 101–108
Crockère, Basile, 66, 77–79

149

Index

Dalcour, Pierre, 12, 34–36
Dalloz, C. J. (Jean Charles Houzheau), 133, 133n
Daquin, Major Louis, 4n, 28n, 81n
Dauphin, Desormes, 51
Davis, Edgar, 118, 199
Deberque, Constantin, 82
Dédé, Edmond, 85–86
Déjour, Julien, 94–95
Delile, Henriette, 99
Demazilière, Formidor, 131, 138
Democratic party, 67, 136
Derham, James D., 77n
Deruise, Donatien, 107
Desbrosses, Nelson, 52–53
Desdunes, Daniel, xvi, 143
Desdunes, Emile, 109, 112–13
Desdunes, P. A., 107n
Desdunes, Rodolphe Lucien, xiii, xiv, xvii, xviii., xix, xxiv, 5n, 43n, 67, 107, 141, 143
Dessalines, Jean Jacques, 8n, 113n
"Deux Ans Après" (poem), 49n
Dostie, A. P., 131, 131n
Dubuclet, Antoine, 74, 75n, 131n
Dueling, 79n
Duelists, 78–79
Duhart, Adolphe, 21, 68, 104
Duhart, Armand, 68, 107
Dumas, François Ernest, 133n
Dunn, Oscar, J., 66n, 115n, 131n
Durant, Thomas J., 130–31

Edmunds, E. J., 72, 73
Emancipation of slaves, 126, 128–29
Emigration of 1858, pp. 109, 112–13
"Épitre á Constant Lépouzé en recevant" (poem), 40
Escoffié, François, 80
Esteves, Arthur, 107, 141, 147–48

Farragut, David G., 118
Faustin I. *See* Soulouque, Faustin I
Federal government, xiii, 119, 121
Fencing, 79n
Fouché, Nelson, 21, 73, 107, 133
France, xxiii, 65n, 68, 72, 73n, 86, 100, 112, 134, 142
Free black battalion, 28, 81n
Free Negroes, 29n, 78, 81, 82, 103n, 104n, 109n, 110, 112

Gallaud, Clovis, 107
Gaudin, Juliette, 99n
Gauthreaux Law, 146
Gautier, J. S. 107
Geffrard, Fabre, 113
Gens de couleur libre, ix, xix, 113n
Georges-Alcès, 90–91
Gibbons, Charles W., 120n
Girodeau, Virginie, 101
Gottschalk, Louis Moreau, 82n, 83
Grant, Ulysses, xxiii, 129
Guimbillotte, Oscar, 75–76
Guirenovich, A. J., 141

Haiti, xviii, xiv, 8n, 53, 65, 81, 94, 112, 113n
Harlan, John, 142, 144
Hayes, Rutherford B., 136
Home for the aged, 92
Home for boys, 92
Hospice of the holy family, 99
Houzheau, Jean Charles (C. J. Dalloz), 133n

Indians, 106n
Inter-Ocean (newspaper), 142

Jackson, Andrew, 3, 4, 81n, 122n
Janssens, Francis X., 145–46
Johnson, Andrew, 124, 127–28, 130
Johnson, G. G., 141
Joubert, L. J., 141
"Justification" (poem), 51

Kellogg, Milliam Pitt, 75n, 136n
Kennedy, A. B., 141

Labat, Alcée, 95, 141
Labat, Emile, 80
L'Abeille de la Nouvelle Orleans, 78n, 85, 100, 109n
L'Athénée Louisianais, 12n

Index

"La Campagne de 1814-15" (poem), 5, 6
Lacoste, Major Pierre, $4n$
Lacroix, François, 21, 99, 103, 104
Lacroix, Mme. François, 99
Lafon, Thomy, 92, 93-94, $102n$, 104, 107, $131n$
Lainez, Louis, 18, 104
La Lorgnette, $43n$
"L'Amant Dédaigne" (poem), 42
"L'Amante du Corsair" (poem), 33
Lamartine, Alphonse M., $10n$, 12, 26, $40n$, 42
Lambert: as prominent New Orleans name, $82n$
Lamotte, Louise R., 83-84, 100
Lanna, J. P., 131
Lanusse, Armand, 6, 10, 11, 13, 14-23, $24n$, 25, 36, 48, 53, 101, 104
Lanusse, Numa, 50-51
Lataure, Séverin, 80
Latour, Arsene, $122n$
La Tribune de la Nouvelle Orleans, 20, 28, $65n$, 66, $67n$, 79, $133n$, 135, 136, 140
"La Vision" (poem), 26
Lavigne-Vigneaux, Joseph, 22, $24n$, 104
"Le Changement" (poem), 48
Le Crusader (newspaper), xvii, $65n$, $67n$, 96, 141, 146, 147
Le Dimanche (newspaper), $43n$
Lee, Robert E., xxiii
LeRay, Francis X., $108n$
"Le Retour de Napoleon" (poem), $29n$, 30-32
Les Cenelles, $6n$, $7n$, 10, 12, 15, 20, 25, 26, $29n$, $33n$, 35, 36, 40, $42n$, 43, $46n$, $49n$, 51-53, $54n$, $56n$, 57, 58, 65, 81
Les Contemporains, 81
Les Vagabonds, $33n$
Lincoln, Abraham, 8, 124, 128, 129
Liotau, F., 54
"L'orphelin des tombeaux" (poem), $43n$, 44-46
Logan, John Alexander, 122
Louisianian, 66

Louisiana Union, the, 68
L'Ouverture, Toussaint, xviii, $8n$
L'Union, $65n$, 66, 104, 132, $133n$
Luscy, Eugène, 107, 141

Macarty, Eugène, 83-85
Macarty, Victor, $131n$
McKinley, William, xv
Manehault, Constantine, 21, $103n$, 104, 105
Mansion, Lucien, (Lolo), 64, $67n$, $90n$
Mansion, Numa E., $67n$, 141
Marigny, Bernard de, 112
Marigny, Orville, 73
Martin, Auguste, 108
Martinet, Louis A., xvii, $67n$, 141, 142, 146, 148
Mary, Aristide, 92-94, $102n$, 104, 107, $131n$, 137, 140, 141
Mercier, Alfred, 11, $12n$
Mercier, Armand, 11, $12n$
Mexico, $65n$, $86n$, 112
Michel, Philip, 107
Monthieu, Leoni, 80
Moore, Thomas Overton, $121n$, 122
Music, 82-85, 87, 89

Negroes: in New Orleans in Spanish regime, x; in West Florida, x; in Louisiana, x, 112, $126n$; in New Orleans in 1812, xii; disfranchisement, discrimination, xv, 130, 137, 142-43; suffrage, $127n$, $131n$, 132; in southern states, 137; mentioned, xviii, 71, 112
Nicholls, Francis Redding Tillou, 136

Ogé, Jacques Vincent, $8n$
Orleans Theater, 68, 82, $83n$
Orso, Edmond, 101

Packard, Stephen B., 115
Pétion, Alexandre Sabès, $8n$
Philanthropists, 90, 92
Pickhil, Alexandre, 71

151

Index

Pinchback, Pinckney Benton Stewart, 66
Piron, M. J., 141
Planciançois, Sergeant, 122n
Plessy v. *Ferguson*, xiii, 144
Populus, August, 49n, 55, 56n
Populus, Mme., 3, 104
Port Hudson, 121, 122n, 125n
Prevost, Eugène, 87

Questy, Joanni, 25–28

Radical Republic Club, 130, 131
Rapp, Eugène, 118, 119
Reconstruction period, xiii, 79, 84, 106n, 107, 115, 120, 127n, 128–29, 131, 136n
"Réponse à mon ami Michel St. Pièrre" (poem), 56
Republican party, xv, 20n, 79, 114, 116, 129, 135
Restoration, 128, 130
Rey, Barthélemy, 21, 114
Rey, Henry L., 114, 118, 119
Rey, Hippolyte, 114
Rey, Octave, 109, 114–20, 122, 123
Reynès, Constant, 22, 24n, 104
Rillieux, Norbert, 59n, 70, 73, 74, 80
Rillieux, Victor Ernest, 59, 80
Riot of September 14, 1874, p. 116
Riot of July 30, 1866, pp. 120n, 127, 131n
"Rondeau Redouble" (poem), 6n, 7, 57
Roosevelt, Theodore, xv
Roudanez, Charles, 130n
Roudanez, Jean B., 130n, 131
Roudanez, Louis Charles, 20n, 66, 131, 133n, 134
Rousseau, Joseph Colastin, 81

Saint Domingue, xi, xvii, 54–55, 113n
St. Louis Cathedral, 69, 103n
St. Mary's Church, New Orleans, 85
St. Pierre, Michel, 48, 49, 55, 56n
St. Sauvinet, Albin, 119, 120
Savary, Joseph, 81

Schools: Bernard Couvent school, 14, 16, 21–23, 68, 101, 102, 104, 106; Home for boys, 92; Nelson Medard, 106n; public, 106n, 137n; sisters of the holy family, 99, 106; sisters of the Holy Ghost, 99, 106n; Southern University, 106n; Straight University, 106n
Slaves, x, xiii, 106n, 110n, 111n, 112, 113, 118, 121, 126n, 140
Snaër, Samuel, 84–85, 104
Société des artisans, 29
Société d'economie, 29, 30
Society [order] of the holy family, 99
"Soudain" (poem), 58
Soudé, Joseph, 115
Soulouque, Faustin I, 109, 112–13
Southern University, 106n, 137
Suffrage, 131, 132
Straight University, 106n
Sugar refining, 59n, 73, 74
Sylva, Manuel, 58

Taxation of Negroes, 106n
Theater of Bordeaux, 85
Théâtre français, 29n
Théâtre Orleans, 87
Thierry, Camille, 32–36
Tissot, A. L., 145, 146
Toucoutou affair, xviii, 61–64
Trevigne, Paul, 66, 67n, 68, 79, 104, 131, 132
Tourgée, Albion W., 141, 142

"Une impression" (poem), 54
Unification movement, 133n, 138
Union, 23, 125n, 128–30, 142
Union army, 118, 122, 124, 125
Ursulines, 106n

Valcour, B., 36, 39–40
Vêque, Charles, 84
"Vision" (poem), 43n

Walker, James, 144
Warbourg, Daniel, 70–71
Warbourg, Eugène, 69–70

Index

Warmoth, Henry Clay, 67n, 114, 115
Wells, J. Madison, 127n
West Indies, xvii, 65n, 73n, 86n
White, Edward Douglas, 75n
Williams, E. A., 141
Wiltz, Louis Alfred, 136

www.ingramcontent.com/pod-product-compliance
Lightning Source LLC
Chambersburg PA
CBHW071425160426
43195CB00013B/1817